The
MomsTown℠
Guide to Getting It All

The MomsTown.sm

Guide to Getting It All

A LIFE MAKEOVER FOR STAY-AT-HOME MOMS

Mary Goulet & Heather Reider

HYPERION NEW YORK

Library of Congress Cataloging-in-Publication Data

Goulet, Mary.
    The MomsTown guide to getting it all : a life makeover for stay-at-home moms / by Mary Goulet & Heather Reider.—1st ed.
        p.   cm.
    Based on the Internet talk radio program MomsTown.
    ISBN 1-4013-0787-6
    1. Mothers. 2. Housewives. 3. Self-realization. 4. Conduct of life. I. Reider, Heather. II. MomsTown (Internet radio program). III. Title.

HQ759.G6298 2005
306.874'3—dc22   2004062552

Hyperion books are available for special promotions and premiums. For details contact Michael Rentas, Assistant Director, Inventory Operations, Hyperion, 77 West 66th Street, 11th floor, New York, New York 10023, or call 212-456-0133.

FIRST EDITION

10 9 8 7 6 5 4 3

306.8743
G

CONTENTS

Introduction   1

WEEK 1: The GAL Starter Tools   13
WEEK 2: The GAL Identity   29
WEEK 3: Get Organized: Get Into the Flow   55
WEEK 4: Getting a Life and a Body Attitude to Match   79
WEEK 5: Mommy Einstein—From Mush to Matter   109
WEEK 6: Getting in Touch with Your Spirituality   135
WEEK 7: The MomsTown Alarm Clock:
         It's Time to Wake Up Your Dreams   171
WEEK 8: Balance: How to Bend Without Breaking
         When You're Pulled in Every Direction   195
WEEK 9: The Virtue of Vanity:
         Why Grandma Wears Lipstick   231
WEEK 10: Powerful and Pockets Full: The MomsTown
         Way to Make, Spend, and Save More Money   249

Conclusion: The MomsTown Way of Life   273
Acknowledgments   275

The MomsTown

Guide to Getting It All

INTRODUCTION

Welcome to MomsTown! If you are a stay-at-home mom who craves an exciting and passionate life, then you're in the right place. You're in the company of moms who have made the decision to pursue their passions and who believe that staying home to raise children is a priority and a gift. At MomsTown we believe stay-at-home moms have an amazing opportunity to create a life for themselves that will help them achieve their dreams.

Being a stay-at-home mom (SAHM) can mean a variety of things. At MomsTown we have developed a program that helps moms who work from home, moms who want to develop businesses out of their homes, and moms who simply want to develop a life that encompasses their passions and dreams, in addition to their traditional roles. At MomsTown, we devote ourselves to our family life *and* we pursue dreams for ourselves. This book is about fulfilling your goals of attaining and developing a passion, a confidence, and a positive inner and outside image as a stay-at-home mom. We will work to recover those secret (or not-so-secret) aspirations that you might have put on the back burner while raising your darling little cherubs. We know you're busy, we know you love your children, but we also know you want to live your life to the fullest. At MomsTown, we show you how to do just that.

MomsTown Philosophy

Being a stay-at-home mom should add to your identity and not take it over. As a mom you've poured your heart and soul into your children; you've made birthday cakes that look like turtles, painted dinosaurs on your child's walls; you've balanced the family budget and despite all your accounting efforts still can't believe how fast the money goes. You've scrubbed grass stains out of your kid's soccer uniform and even managed to calm the raging seas when the first hormonal tantrum of adolescence came screaming from your daughter's mouth. You've got to hand it to yourself: You're a darn good mom.

But lurking somewhere in your heart is a little notion that, hey, this can't be everything. Well, guess what? It isn't. It is an uncomfortable reality that sometimes, while you are staying home and taking care of your brood, one very important thing can get lost: YOU.

"I had a master's degree in communications and was working for a top PR firm in my area when I got pregnant," says Jill, a mother of two. "I had this idealized vision of a carefree existence, free of career responsibility. Well, it turns out, I *like* career responsibility. Finding the perfect fabric softener just wasn't cutting it, but I didn't want to miss watching my kids grow up either." No surprise there. If you have ever been to a playgroup with other stay-at-home moms, you'll be familiar with the litany of complaints: "I'm exhausted . . . My husband doesn't get it—he thinks I'm spoiled and all I do is play all day with the kids . . . I feel unfulfilled . . . I feel antsy . . . I wish I could find a way to make money from home and create an identity for myself again."

Take it from us: It doesn't have to be this way. Staying at home doesn't mean you have to put your own life and personal aspirations on hold while you raise your children. Your growth and your children's growth are not mutually exclusive. If you've already lost some of your spunk to the doldrums of grocery shopping, dropping 'em off and picking 'em up, and scrubbing yet another juice stain out of the carpet, all you need is some help breaking the spin cycle. We have good news: You've picked up the right book. Using the MomsTown program, you are going to figure out what those lost desires are. We're going to help you drag them out of the closet, dust them off, and add them to your daily life as a mother. We're not advocating giving up your Supermom self, only that you remember that the best Supermoms are the ones who are fulfilled—and that means putting yourself first. We guarantee you'll be happier for it. Some of our MomsTown members have businesses from home and are successfully fulfilling their dreams, earning a paycheck, and raising their children. Others are full-time moms who devote themselves to their families but have also figured out how to find their own passions and pursue them. We've done it, countless moms are doing it, and so can you.

We believe getting it all means having a life that is exactly what you want. Having a family and staying home doesn't mean you can't have it all. Some of you have already figured out ways to work out of the home and want to improve your organization and quality of life, while others want to figure out what your passions are and how to take the first step. Regardless of how far along you are, we promise to take you further! We invite you to join the revolution of hip, intelligent, and savvy moms who still know how to read a good bedtime story. We at MomsTown believe you can have your low-carb cake and eat it, too. You can be a spectacular, amazing mother to your children, goddess of the home, and wife to your husband—and you can be the superwoman you always wanted to be. The MomsTown program teaches that you don't have to sacrifice one for the other. Actually, fulfilling your desires to own your own business, play the flute, or create art only makes you more of a fabulous mother. And we can all agree, when Momma ain't happy, ain't nobody happy.

MomsTown Quiz

Below is a short quiz to see if this book is for you. Are you MomsTown material?

1. Do you feel there is something more you'd like to do in your life other than changing diapers and sorting laundry, but you can't quite put your finger on what it is?

2. Do you feel guilty about wanting more, even though you seem to "have it all"?

3. Do you feel guilty for daydreaming about the thrill of the deal and how you can create it again while home with your kids?

4. Do you miss earning a paycheck?

5. Do you ever feel you've lost your edge?

6. Do you sometimes wonder if your IQ has dropped with each child you've had?

7. Do you have your own budding business from home but can't quite figure out how to bring it to the next level of success *and* keep up your household duties?

8. If you could get yourself to a cocktail party, do you fear you wouldn't have anything of substance to talk about?

9. Do your breasts feel as if they are filled with pancake batter?

10. Do you fear you'll never get into a bikini again?

11. Do you feel like the last intellectual adventure you went on was trying to calculate your due date?

12. Do you want more excitement in life than a new *SpongeBob SquarePants* episode?

13. Are you feeling antsy or restless and do you find yourself wondering what more you could be doing with your life?

14. Do you feel invisible, as if the only people who see you are your kids or husband—and then only when they need something?

15. Do you feel more like a servant than a goddess?

16. Do you feel your "hippest" years are behind you?

If you answered yes to more than three of the above questions, you may be suffering from the stay-at-home itch! In this book we will provide you with the basic tools and knowledge to achieve what you want in life, get motivated, find inspiration, and just plain get it all. MomsTown will give you a blueprint for how to get everything you're dreaming of and more. So gear up: You're about to get a life!

Getting It All Will Make You a "Gal"

We're all "Gals" at MomsTown—that is, we're working on Getting A Life. We have discovered getting it all can do wonders not only for ourselves but also for our families. Throughout our program we use the acronym GAL, for Get a Life, to describe the transformation that happens when a mom has her own life, pursues her own passions in addition to raising her children. Gals have it all. It's that simple. A Gal becomes her own person—outside the identity of being a stay-at-home mom (SAHM). Getting a Life means finding your passion, your dreams, making it through your daily routine with more energy and confidence. In the process, you become an official MomsTown Gal.

Getting everything you want out of life and becoming a Gal can entail changes in your routine and outlook on countless levels. At MomsTown we've created a solid, accessible program to help you get what you want in life. In our experience, talking with countless moms, we have found that deciding to change your life in an abstract sense isn't enough. A step-by-step plan is the only way for a busy mom to make changes in her life. We have found that moms who attempt to make massive changes without a program or support group can get frustrated and eventually discouraged. The greatest advantage to the MomsTown program is that it shows you how to take a detailed, practical approach to your life in a strategic way that adds up to overall change and positive lifestyle results. The program focuses on getting it all, which in MomsTown terms means feeling confident, having a great attitude about yourself, and feeling good about your image, body, health, and spirituality. We have developed a program women across the country have experienced with phenomenal success. Here are just a few benefits women have found after doing the MomsTown program:

- A new attitude, self-image, and confidence
- More energy and a great sense of achievement at the end of the day
- A healthier, fitter lifestyle and a body to match
- A more confident parenting style
- The sense of being a better role model for their children

- A healthier and more fun sex life
- A more passionate daily routine and the energy to devote to it

OUR STORY
Heather

I am a wife, mother, daughter, sister, friend, and business partner. I have three sons and am a stay-at-home mom (or SAHM, as we say at MomsTown). Before children I had a thriving career in broadcast journalism and worked for CBS, NBC, and ABC affiliates in the western states. I loved my career and enjoyed the sense of purpose it gave me, but I had always wanted to have children and stay home to care for them.

I had my first child during my first year of marriage and left my job to stay at home with him. Being home every day with my first baby was an incredible experience. I felt very lucky to be able to stay home and I was in complete baby mode—so much so I had two more babies within the next three years. In fact, I spent five years either pregnant or nursing.

However, when I was pregnant with my third, I started to get "the itch." I felt like I had mommyhood mastered, but what about my womanhood?

I started seeking out other moms for social interaction, in an attempt to find my place and understand how other moms dealt with these restless feelings.

I wrestled with the identity that I, and most of society, had always associated with the label of "stay-at-home-mom." My stereotypical image of SAHMs had always been that they were matronly, kind, and devoted to their children. Images of SAHMs filled the media. When I watched TV I saw moms who did a dance when they cleaned their toilet bowl or flashed bright smiles because their carpets were exceptionally clean. Their identities seemed to reside in keeping house.

That image of a woman devoted to cleaning her house and taking care of her children—that and that alone—did not resonate within me. I did want my home to be clean and my children to be well cared for. But I also knew I wanted an identity that was my own, outside of being a SAHM.

My personal experience as a mother led me to MomsTown. I began to search everywhere for the SAHM identity that I could identify with. I went online and looked at mom sites and SAHM sites. I had difficulty finding one that honored an identity outside of taking care of your children.

I finally resolved to create my own site where moms who want to be more than just a SAHM could go. The women I wanted to focus on were moms who want to be hip, savvy, independent, and outgoing about their personal goals and passions, along with being great homemakers and mothers. I created the MomsTown Web site and the motto "Where Hip Moms Click." The response to my Web site reaffirmed what I believed about most mothers: Moms do want to identify themselves as hip, savvy, sexy, and fun, and not women who get excited over clean toilets. Many of us just aren't sure how to get the image out there.

Since then, I have had a phenomenal response from women who want to do more and have their own identity. When I teamed up with Mary, we developed a program that walks moms through the step-by-step approach we learned ourselves, to getting a life and an identity all their own. MomsTown has evolved into a popular Web site and Internet talk radio show. In my partnership with Mary, MomsTown also has expanded nationwide, with a network of local town sites coming online. We are growing at an exciting pace.

The commitment to my own life is the best commitment I have ever made. I have a great marriage and three exuberant boys, and lead an exciting life as a wife, mother, and entrepreneur.

I have found my dream of having children, a husband, and a career from home has been instrumental in not only my family's happiness and health but also my own. I am a better mom when I'm myself.

My hope is that all women who visit MomsTown, through this book or the Web site format, leave with an idea for following their passions. It's my belief that motherhood makes us better. It teaches us unconditional love, patience, and humility. And within each of us is inherent strength and determination. All mothers want exceptional lives for their children. We should teach by example and lead exceptional lives ourselves. But to manage this, we must support and encourage each other. That is what MomsTown does.

Mary

I am a wife, the mother of two girls, and a passionate entrepreneur. I have many interests and believe my life truly began when I had my children. I began my career on Wall Street. After nine successful years I moved to California and opened a real estate company. I met my husband and had my children, and decided I didn't want to conform to many of the societal pressures and stereotypes that SAHMs face. I believed I could have it all: staying home with my kids and earning a paycheck, as well as continuing to grow and develop the many interests I had.

After having my first child, I wanted to stay at home and did not want to work in a corporate environment any longer, but I did want the financial perks of a successful career. There was a prevalent belief among the people I worked with that was condescending toward SAHMs and anyone outside of the corporate structure. In my world as a stay-at-home mom, I missed the entrepreneurial aspects of business. I decided to take the risk and try my hand at business from the home as I took care of my children. I also wanted to instill hope in women and prove that they, too, can create the life they want and break through the social barriers placed in front of women who stay home. This surprised many of my former colleagues, especially women who had children themselves, who were afraid to venture outside of the corporate world and risk their salaries and their credibility as career-oriented businesswomen. There was no precedent for SAHMs, or women who left the corporate safety net, to blossom as independent entrepreneurs.

It bothered me that you weren't supposed to be a successful businesswoman on your own. I disagreed with many of my friends who had remained at jobs they disliked because they believed it wasn't an option to stay with their kids and still have business potential. They didn't see an identity outside of the corporate world, but I did. I developed a passion to succeed and to prove to my Wall Street friends that I could make a living staying home with my children, away from the office and out from behind the desk.

My past success on Wall Street and subsequent success owning my own real estate company empowered me and made me feel anything was possible. I decided I wanted to get into motivational speaking and went to a seminar with my now mentor and business coach, Mark LeBlanc, and I got involved in radio and began the *Entrepreneur Magazine Home-based Business Show,* which focused on having your own business from home. Many of my listeners were SAHMs from around the world who wanted to start their own businesses but had no direction as to how to do it. The show focused on operating a business from home utilizing technology and online resources. It became a great success and began to gather a following. When I met Heather we decided to combine our efforts and launched the MomsTown Internet radio program. Since then, we have developed a network of women across the country who want their own goals, identity, and success, outside of being mothers. I am an advocate for women who want to be their best selves. I believe in the inherent creative power women possess. When Heather and I first met, we agreed instantly that if women have the power to create a life in forty weeks even while sleeping, imagine what they can create with their lives while they are awake! That is our core message. Women are creative, powerful, resourceful, and wise, and they can create a life in which they get it all. At MomsTown, we are excited to show them how!

Ten Weeks of Teachings—a Lifetime of MomsTown

This program is divided into ten weeks. Each week, we will introduce you to a new level of the program and will carry over the teachings of the previous week. In ten weeks, we believe you can establish a firm foundation on which to build your new life. In ten weeks, we will present our practical steps toward overcoming issues moms face as they juggle kids, family, work, and their inner and outer images. We will walk you through the basic steps that evolved as we did the program ourselves. We are living examples: If we could do it—so can you! Our MomsTown program teaches women how to uncover their identities and passions. We welcome you to a new way of discovering your passions and your dreams.

WEEK 1: THE GAL STARTER TOOLS

There are a few basic tools you will need as you follow your path toward the GAL lifestyle. Like so many moms who have participated in our program, workshops, and seminars, you will come to rely on these tools—they form the foundation of this program.

TOOL # 1: **The GAL Commitment**

Your commitment to your new life is fundamentally necessary. Sign the commitment on page 15 and allow yourself to make a firm, non-negotiable pact with yourself. You deserve to devote energy to yourself, and this GAL Commitment reinforces your pledge to do so.

TOOL # 2: **Make Your Bed!**

This may seem very simple because it is. *Make your bed every day.* It's that easy. Beginning a day with the bed made is like beginning a book with the introduction and the first chapter under your belt. By making your bed first thing in the morning, you get your day off to the right start.

Every morning during Week 1, we ask you to make your bed immediately after rising. Make this the very first thing you do. You will continue this practice throughout the rest of the program and beyond.

Below is our step-by-step guide on how we make our beds at MomsTown. Even if you think you know how to make your bed, follow our basic instructions, because it's not just a list of directions—it is a MomsTown ritual.

1 Take all the covers, the cover sheet, and the pillows (and your kids' toys) off the bed.

2 Straighten out the bottom sheet and make it smooth, with no wrinkles or lumps. Draw it tight on both sides, tucking it under if need be.

3 Take the cover sheet and flip it up in the air, allowing it to come down evenly over the bed and smoothing any parts that do not. Allow for a foot and a half (depending on your mattress size) past the foot of the bed and tuck it under, making sure that at least five inches are under the mattress.

4 Make hospital bed corners on the sides.

5 Make sure the cover sheet is drawn tight and smooth.

6 Take the spread and smooth it over the whole bed, making sure it is even on either side and at the foot of the bed.

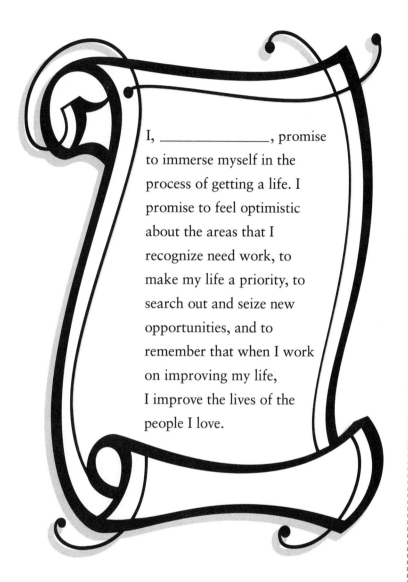

I, _____, promise to immerse myself in the process of getting a life. I promise to feel optimistic about the areas that I recognize need work, to make my life a priority, to search out and seize new opportunities, and to remember that when I work on improving my life, I improve the lives of the people I love.

7 Take the pillows and place them at the head of the bed and fluff them gently.

8 Step back and take an admiring view of the bed itself.

Good work! You will find a sense of accomplishment greets you at the beginning of your day. Not only will you feel more organized, you will also have a sense of clarity every time you go in and out of your bedroom, and especially when you go to bed at night. For SAHMs who spend a good deal of time in their home, it is very important to keep the place organized. The state of your house reflects your state of mind. Making your bed first thing begins the cycle of the day on a positive note.

One of our MomsTown members, Luciana, who has been making her bed every day for the past six months, says, "It just makes my morning feel so much more organized. I love coming into my bedroom and seeing my bed made nicely. I invested in some nice pillows in my favorite colors, and the bedroom became my favorite room in the whole house. I used to avoid going in my bedroom because the bed was not made. Now forgetting to make it is not an option. I love sitting on it to read when the kids are taking a nap."

Your Bed Is More Than a Bed

Remember, when you make your bed, it is not just about being prim and proper. Your bed is where you rest, regroup, dream, make love, and make babies; that is why making your bed is important. It's a task that requires little thought. As you make your bed, allow yourself to think about your upcoming day. During this time, prep yourself for your day, allow yourself to dream, come up with creative ways for getting through your day and getting tasks done. This ritual can be meditative as you close out one day and begin another.

TOOL # 3: **The Buddy System: Finding Your Ethel**

When we began to develop this program, we found that we relied heavily on each other for moral support. If one of us doesn't stick to our workouts, schedules, or diary entries, the other knew and would remind us of our GAL Commitment. Just as Lucy in *I Love Lucy* had Ethel, that is what Heather is to Mary and Mary is to Heather—we are each other's Ethels!

Think for a moment if you have a friend who is a SAHM like you. Do you know someone who has the same lingering desire for a little— or a lot—more? This is someone who may be a great buddy and who would benefit by doing the program herself. By bringing a new MomsTown member into the program, you are helping a friend. Finding a buddy to commit to the program and check in with throughout each week is a huge help to you as well. Find an Ethel you can call your own and ask her if she will do the MomsTown program with you.

If someone comes to mind immediately and fits the profile of a SAHM who wants to get a life, don't be shy! Pick up the phone and call her. Do it today. Chances are, if she is the right Gal to be your Ethel, she will be thrilled to find there is a program specifically for SAHMs who want it all—who doesn't find that exciting? One of our MomsTown members, Jean, said of her buddy, "My buddy is another SAHM who is always there when I need to call and complain about my schedule, relate my newest potty training crisis, or just have a good laugh. I don't know what I would do without her. She is my support in the smallest and largest ways."

Some criteria to consider when choosing a buddy:

- Find a buddy who passes the 3 A.M. test. If you can call this friend at 3 A.M. in case of an emergency, that's a real Ethel for you. If you haven't gotten to that point with this friend, but trust her and think you may at some point—she is an option for a buddy.

- Find a buddy with whom you feel comfortable discussing your triumphs, successes, frustrations, and dilemmas. Make sure you feel that this friend is supportive of you.

- Find a buddy you can be honest and open with.

- Find a buddy who supports you rather than judges you.

- Find a buddy who works at the same speed as you do. You should have matching energy levels.

- Avoid a buddy who makes you feel you must act a certain way or be something you are not.

- Avoid a buddy who seems to always have a drama that takes over every discussion or meeting you have with her.

Along with your Ethel, remember—we are right here with you! At MomsTown, you have a whole network of moms available online.

If you don't have a buddy and you can't seem to find the right fit for your Ethel, that is no excuse not to begin the program. Go for it anyway! If you find a buddy along the way, incorporate her. When it comes down to it, this is about you and your life. So with or without a buddy, let's get started!

TOOL # 4: The GAL Diary

We at MomsTown believe diaries aren't just for little girls. One of the most important tools in our program is a diary. You may remember that journal you had growing up; this is going to be very similar. Go out and buy yourself a diary. Use your imagination as you choose one that speaks to you—one that you enjoy writing in. You are allowed to have any color you like. Here are some things to keep in mind while you shop for the perfect journal.

1 Chose a diary that reminds you of your taste as a little girl. You may even want to go to the kids' section (you know where it is!) and pick one that speaks to your inner Gal. It doesn't have to be sophisticated, elegant, or refined, unless you prefer that. You are allowed any design your heart desires. If your favorite color is pink, or you are drawn to the diary with the rainbow or purple sparkles—go for it!

2 Choose one with lined pages.

3 Locks are optional.

4 You don't have to tell anyone you are doing this, not even your husband!

As soon as you get this diary, cut out the GAL Commitment on page 15 with a pair of scissors, take some Elmer's glue, and paste it into the first page of your diary. This pledge marks the beginning of your new identity, so it's important to refer to it regularly. By pasting it in your journal you will see the GAL Commitment every time you open its pages to make an entry.

In this diary, you are going to confide your deepest hopes, fears, expectations, dreams, daily dramas, and best of all, your big and small successes. This will be where you discover your passions! You will use this diary for particular exercises throughout the book. Your diary will be where you record your commitments, and your success in following through on them.

The GAL Diary Duty

As moms, we realize that writing seven days a week is a tall order. But at least three days a week, you must write an update in your GAL Diary about your work toward Getting A Life. Your entry should be around two pages long each time. We suggest you write on Mondays, Wednesdays, and Fridays, but you can choose the days that work best with your schedule. These three days serve as tent posts for the rest of the week, holding a structure for other days to rest on. Because you will be required to write only three days a week, make sure you stick to it. Write more if you can, but be faithful to those three days.

One of our MomsTown members, Ann, says of her diary: "Journaling helps me solve problems, see solutions more clearly, and take an objective look at some of the chatter in my head. It is a nice way to review my day. I find it very rewarding."

Pick a time of the day when this works for you. Perhaps it is in the morning or in the evening. Whatever you decide, stick to it. This is your time and you must honor it.

Along with regular entries, there will be "GAL-ercises" that ask you to do an exercise in your diary. Writing in your diary provides a quiet, creative space for you to get to know your inner Gal.

TOOL # 5: The GAL Mantra

There will be times—you know about these moments—of great frustration and discouragement. It can be challenging to raise children, nurture a relationship with your husband, maintain a social life, and achieve your dramatic and ultimate goddess-like potential as a woman. We have faith you can do it, but for those times when you need some extra help, we offer you the GAL Mantra.

Mantras are phrases that are spoken—either verbally or internally—and help promote spiritual strength and peace. Our GAL Mantra is what we will call on when we hit the roof, when we think we have had enough and can't take anymore, or when we simply need to remember why we go to the trouble of getting a life.

During this program there will be trying times when you will need to access your inner core and strength. The GAL Mantra will help you with that.

In this first week of the program, we ask you to develop a mantra to say when you reach the boiling point. You may choose one of the mantras below or create your own. You can use these if they make you feel empowered and ready to Get a Life. Try them out and see which ones work for you. Some of these have become lifesavers for moms who have done our program.

I am worthy of complete happiness.
I have the potential to be everything I dream of being.
I am a confident, passionate, deserving woman.
I am inherently creative and powerful.

If you are creating your own, here are a few guidelines.

* It should be no longer than ten words.

* It should be easy to remember so you can recall it in times of stress or anxiety.

* When said aloud or mentally, it should invoke peace and a feeling of empowerment.

* You don't have to tell your husband, children, or even your buddy what your GAL Mantra is. It is yours and yours alone!

* As soon as you have decided on your GAL Mantra (or chosen one of ours above), write it on the second page of your diary, right after the GAL Commitment you have pasted on the first page.

* Take a moment to find a quiet spot, close your eyes, clear your mind, and repeat the GAL Mantra three times.

Julie found that her six-year-old had learned to push her buttons when she was trying to keep to her schedule. He would find diversions and figure out ways to get her attention, often by throwing a fit when Julie was on the way to run an errand, get to an aerobics class, or get him to school on time. At these moments she would say the GAL Mantra she had created for herself: "I am in charge of the schedule and am doing the best I can. I am giving it my all." After saying her mantra, she would take a deep breath and reassess in a cool, collected way.

Eventually her son began to see it was tougher to ruffle her feathers and started cooperating more.

TOOL # 6: **The GAL Truths**

In embracing the following truths, you make a paradigm shift that reveals your best self. The GAL Truths are universal. Accepting these truths will set you up for success. Once you understand and internalize these truths you can move forward, leaving behind your negative beliefs and self-imposed limitations.

You come first. When you're on an airplane and the flight attendant is going over the safety instructions, what are you told to do in case of an emergency? You place the oxygen mask on *your* face first, and *then* assist your child. Using that as a metaphor, as women we must take care of ourselves first so we are better equipped to care for our families. This doesn't mean others are last, it means you have to take care of yourself to give the best care to your children.

Money is important. We're taught that wanting more money is greedy and unattractive, and it *can* be if people and values are sacrificed in the effort. But the fact is, money buys freedom and privilege. If you never admit out loud that you want and deserve more money, you'll never have it. It's easier to handle the daily stresses of life when you're not worried about paying the bills. In this book we will address your money hang-ups and how to change your financial reality. No matter what your socio-economic class, you will benefit from the money chapter.

To get more time, get busy. The old saying goes, "If you want to get something done, give it to a busy person." Busy people have a way of finding time in their day. We know you're busy. You're a mom. We will show you how to thrive on fifteen-minute intervals a day.

To get more energy, get moving. A mom's day never begins or ends. You are on call twenty-four hours a day, seven days a week, 365 days a year. Isn't it great to be in demand? It's a job you can't get fired from. However, moms often overextend themselves and run out of energy. We are going to give you energy-boosting ideas and techniques to make sure you have enough left over for yourself.

To be more creative, take a risk. Our instinct as mothers is to protect and care for our children, and at times this aversion to risk can spill over into other areas of our lives. We can be so protective that we don't take any chances. But when we're always staying in the comfort zone, we lose our edge. The most successful people in this world don't let the possibility of failure stop them. They take risks! The bigger the risk, the bigger the payoff. We will show you how to wean yourself off the safety net and really experience life, risks and all.

Moms are the pulse of the family, community, and economy. It is a powerful position. Moms are the glue that binds the family to the community. We hold control of the heartstrings and the purse strings. We work in the schools and with civic organizations. Moms also make 80 percent of all household purchasing decisions. We are a force to be reckoned with! Accept your influence with gratitude and reverence.

The buddy system works. Women need each other. Women who have girlfriends, sisters, moms, and other women in their lives have strength. They have a shoulder to cry on, and someone to commiserate with. But there's a catch: You only want women in your life who will support you and cheer you on. A real friend or advocate will hold you accountable. She will tell you when you're right and won't abandon you when you're wrong.

You can have it all; you just can't do it all. Even though we have the ability to do many things at once, we don't have the ability to do everything. Accepting help is not an admission of failure. It's being smart enough to recognize your own limitations. It's true that someone else might not do things exactly the way you would, but at least those things are getting done. Delegation is the key, and you don't have to control everything all the time. Delegate to your husband and children.

Husbands don't get it—let it go. Husbands will never understand what it's like to be a mother—the instincts, the demands, the time, the energy, the worry, and the connection to your children. They have their own relationship with the children that you'll never understand. Let go of frustration over the fact that he doesn't see everything exactly your way. This doesn't mean that we let the men out of housework or parenting, but that we acknowledge they might handle things differently sometimes, and we admit to ourselves that we cannot control their behavior. Focus on other aspects of your relationship. It's not right to try to convert him into the role of mother (that's your position).

You can achieve greatness. You just have to work at it. Identify it, believe in yourself, and expect obstacles. Visualize yourself rising above the stress, the details of daily household upkeep, and the traps of a SAHM routine. Look at failure as an indicator of pending success. Look at success as an indicator of more good things to come.

These truths are staples to our philosophy at MomsTown. We will direct you back to them in the coming weeks. You can also return to them if you hit stressful parts of your day and need a reality check. Reading through the above periodically is a great way to remember who you are and what you stand for!

TOOL # 7: This Book

We have specifically designed this book in sections that are short and can be read quickly. Take this book with you in your purse or car and read a section as you wait for an appointment or during a brief break in the day. We are your life coaches—keep us by your side or within close reach. The MomsTown advice, which has been helpful for so many women in our seminars and workshops and on our radio show, is here for you when you need it. Keep us as a resource when you feel frustrated and need a boost. That's why MomsTown was built!

WEEK 1 SUMMARY

Week 1 is about getting your basic tools in order. If you did find a buddy right away, call that buddy and check in. See that you both have covered the list that follows. If you haven't, go down the list and make sure you can check off all of the items from Week 1.

1. Start each day this week with the MomsTown ritual of Tool #2: making the bed.

2. Buy a diary and write at least three days this week—we recommend Monday, Wednesday, and Friday.

3. Sign the GAL Commitment, cut the page out, and paste it to the first page of your GAL Diary.

4. If you haven't found a buddy by the end of this first week, continue with the program on your own and keep looking for your Ethel.

5. Develop a GAL Mantra that works for you, and practice it every time you feel stress, anxiety, or depression.

6. After you read this chapter, read over the GAL Truths once more.

7. If you missed any of these, be forgiving! You can't do everything right the first time. Be patient but consistent in your work as you integrate this program into your daily life.

WEEK 2: THE GAL IDENTITY

One of the first things we're going to ask you to do in the MomsTown program is decide who you are and who you want to be. Being a SAHM is a unique identity unto itself. Whether you have a business that you conduct from your home or your sole business is taking care of your children, you probably struggle with the old ideas about the roles of moms, traditional SAHMs and working moms. In Week 2, we will pinpoint who you have become in your role as a SAHM and who you want to become as a Gal.

No longer are moms in two camps, working moms vs. stay-at-home moms. For too long, SAHMs have lived with the myth that they don't work—when in fact we are some of the hardest-working people on the planet! We believe all SAHMs are working moms. Some of us just don't get a paycheck. However, if you want to blend your role as a SAHM and a WAHM (work-at-home mom) and earn a paycheck too, please keep reading. We're going to teach you how.

Servant or Goddess

Isis was the Egyptian goddess of magic, love, and transformation. She was the goddess of medicine, wisdom, and women who worked in the home. She is said to have spent time with her people and taught women how to grind corn, weave cloth, and tame men enough to live with them. This tells us she had truly magical powers! She became the personification of the "complete female" for the Egyptians. In one story, she disguised herself as a servant in order to catch her philandering husband. Isis reminds us of the inherent power we have. We can be goddesses in so many areas of our life, yet often we let ourselves sink into servitude. As you go through this chapter and assess where you are and where you want to be, ask yourself, Am I a goddess or a servant? In case you've been a servant so long you don't know the difference anymore, here are some guidelines. When you take on the role of a servant, you:

- do not have a firm sense of self
- do not feel empowered
- do not feel in control
- do not have confidence
- do not have a positive attitude
- feel energy is being taken from you

When you take on the role of a goddess, you:

- are confident
- are empowered
- feel sure of the decisions you make
- feel sure about who you are and what you believe
- feel that anything is possible

- are sure of your inherent creativity
- feel passionate about your life

Use these roles of servant and goddess to figure out where you stand on your path toward getting it all. At MomsTown, we believe every woman can be a goddess; it's just a matter of taking a step-by-step approach toward boosting your goals and your self-confidence.

Time and Energy

Being a mom can be tiring. Moms have so much to do. There is a difference between being tired but happy at the end of a long day and the kind of exhaustion that pervades your soul and leaves you wishing for bedtime. Which kind of tired are you? Rate how familiar some of these descriptions are from 1 to 10. Give it a 10 if you always feel this way, a 1 if you never do.

- You feel exhausted at the end of the day and want to run away from everything._____
- You feel that you don't have time for any activity that is solely for you._____
- You feel overwhelmed, like you can never get everything done._____
- You feel resentful because sometimes your family doesn't seem to notice your constant efforts._____
- You feel guilt that you have feelings of resentment and frustration._____

Review your ratings. Are you a goddess or a servant overall?

We believe you can avoid unnecessary exhaustion, fatigue, and the ever-present drained feeling that so many women have. Start by re-assessing your daily commitments.

Learn the power of no.

If you've already volunteered as a chaperone three times in the past year for your children's school, or offered to run the auction committee for the past two years, you can probably say no the next time someone calls you to help with either. Give yourself a break. And don't feel guilty. You've got to fit *you* somewhere in your busy day. This week, pick one thing you feel obligated to do, and say no—even if you don't have a particular event or other obligation that legitimately interferes. During the time you were supposed to be fulfilling whatever obligation you said no to, treat yourself to a bath, some quiet time, or writing in your journal.

Make sure you are enjoying your time with your children—not wishing it away.

Our friend Donna said to us the other day, "I can't wait for Tommy and Jennifer's bedtime at eight. That's when my day starts!" This is a very common experience for moms, but it doesn't have to be. Let's consider this for a moment. Without realizing it, Donna is wishing away her time with her children! You can find the time to take advantage of your day with your children, to cherish their daily experiences, and still have some time to yourself before 8 P.M. Later in the book, we will show you how to find more quality time with your children and be less stressed.

Stay at Homework: Today take ten to fifteen minutes to sit with your children, whether they're playing, sleeping, or eating, and focus on how much you treasure your time with them. Repeat to yourself whenever you wish it were bedtime or babysitter time: "I will never have this moment back and I am enjoying it right now, as it exists."

Guilt and Fear

As moms we have very high standards for ourselves, but we worry about what other people are expecting, what our children and husbands are expecting, what the PTA is expecting—and we try not to disappoint. When we try to meet everyone's expectations and we don't succeed, we feel guilt. And we feel fear. We worry that we are not good moms and that we're not doing enough. In this scenario, we are neither taking care of our-selves nor staying present in our children's lives. As moms we can fall vic-tim to unproductive, soul-breaking self-criticism with the added pressure of raising children. Beware of the voices in your head that want to beat your inner Gal down for not having done enough for others. Simply refuse to listen to those voices and recognize guilt and fear as the Gal's nemesis.

The Assessment: Are you a servant to guilt and fear?

Take a moment and check in with yourself. Do any of the following scenarios sound familiar? Do this exercise like the one above, using 1 to 10 as a measure for how frequently you feel this way. Give the descrip-tion a 10 if you always feel this way, a 1 if you never do.

- If your child is behind in school, is not the star soccer player, or doesn't have enough friends attending her birthday party, you immediately wonder what you might have done to con-tribute to this situation._____
- When you're away from your kids you feel guilty._____
- If you're spending a lot of time with your kids and not your hus-band, you feel guilty._____

- You look around and your house is a mess, and you feel like it should be more well kept._____
- You are afraid you are not doing enough for your kids._____
- You are afraid your kids will not need you at some point. _____
- You act out of fear of not being a good-enough mother. _____
- You act out of guilt for not being the perfect mother or woman to your children, husband, family, and friends._____

Review your ratings. Are you a goddess or a servant overall? If you lean toward servant status, you have fallen into a very common mental pattern. Many moms become absorbed in being a great mother and rarely put time toward their own well-being. This is normal, but not necessary— and certainly not healthy!

Feelings such as guilt and fear are zapping your energy and your focus. You must learn to cut them out of your life as much as possible. They are perfectly natural feelings, but you do not need to allow them to rule your life.

Stay at Homework: During Week 2, one of your assignments is to begin noticing every time you feel guilt or fear. When you do have a tremor of guilt or fear, step back and do the following:

- Take a deep breath and slowly exhale.

- Say your GAL Mantra. Reassure yourself you are doing the best you can.

- Make a mental note that you are feeling guilt or fear and write about the incident in your GAL Diary during your next GAL Diary Duty.

Again, be aware. When you feel the guilt and fear rising, take a breath and see these feelings for what they are. Tell that "Anti-Gal" to take a hike. Remember that this is your show and you are doing the best you can. And guilt and fear should never run your life. Only once you begin to notice how often they rule your life, and begin to divorce yourself from them, will you begin to move toward being a better mom and one heck of a Gal!

The Gal vs. the Joneses

One of the things we began to notice as we were working with SAHMs was the overwhelming pressure that some moms feel to keep up with their friends, neighbors, neighbor's kids, and so on. This can be a major obstacle in your own quest to get a life. Simply being aware of your tendency to keep up with the Joneses is the first step toward cutting this bad habit.

A client of ours has a son who was admitted into one of the best private schools in Southern California. She was telling us that she really believed the violin lessons and weekly Spanish lessons she had recently added to her son's schedule had contributed to his acceptance. Prior to these additions, his only extracurriculars had been three different sports and a budding appreciation of chess. She continued feverishly, telling us that she and her husband believed that you must pursue these demanding, tight schedules for children to succeed and excel in their lives. She listed a group of mothers from whom she had learned all of the tricks of overbooking her son's schedule so he could meet the demands of the school standards.

As she told her story, we wondered how often her son got to just spend time with his parents instead of being carted around to a million different after-school activities that, at the age of five, he probably wasn't even sure he was interested in yet. We wondered if our friend really believed this was best, or whether she was simply trying to keep up with her group of friends who had given her the down and dirty on the best schools and how to get in.

We also discussed what we did at the age of five in our own kindergarten classes: drawing, napping, and finger painting our dads' T-shirts. Our friend bragged to us that the famed private-school kindergarten class would begin with math, science, and a foreign language.

We asked our client to do the following assessment. When she completed it, she was amazed at how often her actions were motivated by others' standards and expectations, and not her own.

The Assessment: Are you a servant to the Joneses?

Take a moment and check in with yourself. Do any of the following scenarios sound familiar? Do this exercise like the servant-or-goddess worksheet on page 33, using 1 to 10 as a measure for how frequently you feel this way. Again, remember 10 is always and 1 is never.

- You worry that your kid(s) will not do as well as their friends (or your friends' kids) in class. _____
- You feel pressure to participate in new, trendy parenting clubs, even though you feel you're a good parent as it stands now. _____
- You worry that your baking for the party at your kids' school is not up to snuff or as creative as the other moms'. _____
- You feel pressure to make sure your kids get all of the right extracurricular activities that their friends do (soccer, T-ball, Mommy & Me, piano lessons, etc.). _____

Review your ratings. Are you a goddess or a servant overall? Other moms and families can be a great support for you as you raise your children, but often that support crosses over into peer pressure from other parents and becomes an extra burden you don't need.

While we admire parents who want to develop their children's extracurricular activities and get them into the best possible school, we can't help but notice a growing trend in our society today toward exclusivity and competitiveness. Books like the *Nanny Diaries* top the bestseller lists, as schools get more and more cutthroat with admittance to kindergarten and even preschool. Parents are led to believe that if they don't jam-pack their kids' lives with tons of worldly music, language, and special development courses, their children will "never become anything" or "never get into the right college."

Next time you feel yourself rushing to sign your child up for a class or camp, or thinking about participating in a neighborhood parenting function, check in with yourself and ask:

- Do I genuinely think this will benefit my child and my family?

- Does my child want to participate in this activity?

- Do I believe this is a good use of my time and my child's time?

- Does this authentically speak to my beliefs about parenting?

At MomsTown, we ask mothers to come back to what they authentically believe is good for their children. At what price are we sacrificing our children's childhoods, imaginations, playtime, and most important, time with us? At what price are we sacrificing our own values and hopes for our children because "everyone else is doing it"? This program is about uncovering why you do what you do and making more time for the things that genuinely matter. As you learn how to discover your own sense of self, you will develop the confidence to stand up and say what you believe. Watch the competitive drive that so many moms fall into when they are raising their children. Take your son to his violin lesson because he likes it, not because you are afraid that without it he won't get into the prep school your neighbor said was the best.

◆ Tips for Avoiding the "Keepin' Up" Blues ◆

- Idle chitchat with other mothers can be a dangerous thing. Standing around at preschool and hearing everyone else's philosophies on motherhood is a good social activity, but if you haven't formed a strong sense of identity in your parenting style, it can introduce a whole host of insecurities about your own abilities as a mom. While we need to connect with other women who do the same things we do, we need support, not pressure from others as to the right or wrong ways to raise children.

- Remind yourself of what you know in your heart. You have your own convictions about what is right for your children. Relax and enjoy being a mother, instead of looking sideways at what other mothers or families are doing. Don't run yourself ragged meeting others' expectations and standards. Once you succumb to competitiveness or standards that are not yours, it becomes labor. Your job as a mother should not be labor—it should be love! One of our MomsTown members, Susie, said of her friends, "There is a big trend to take your kids to tons of extracurricular activities, and sometimes I feel like even though my son doesn't like soccer or whatever sport is the trend, I am depriving him if I don't force him to do it. Finally I decided to do only one

to two well-chosen activities per semester and it has made a huge difference in my sanity, and my son is enjoying the activities more."

♦ Admit what you know deep down: that your children would rather spend quality time with you than be driven around according to a breakneck schedule of extracurricular activities. The more you are sure of the things you believe, the more your family is sure of their values. You are the foundation and backbone. Don't let societal opinions or competitive accomplishments sway your beliefs about how you raise your children. Avoid being a servant to others' opinions. After all—you're a goddess!

Stay at Homework: This week evaluate the long- and short-term soci appointments and commitments you have made for yourself and yo children. This might include their extracurricular activities, weekly pl; dates, volunteer activities, etc. Make a list of them in your GAL Di and carefully evaluate each one. Which ones do you authentically beli are good uses of your family's time? Which ones are there because feel obligated or pressured to include them?

The Hubby

When you are dividing your time among the kids, friends, ch daily obligations, and your husband, things can get hectic, and ; end of the day, it can be difficult to connect with your husband, wh been in a different world. We don't have to tell you your husba partner doesn't necessarily understand what you go through ir daily routine; you probably experience his ignorance on a regular Sometimes a lack of communication can lead to feeling as if he (appreciate the work and stress you deal with day to day.

The Assessment: Are you a servant to your husband?

Do this exercise as you did the above assessment exercises, using 1 to 10 as a measure for how frequently you feel this way. Again, use 10 for always and 1 for never.

- Sometimes you feel resentful because your husband doesn't have to help your son go to the bathroom unexpectedly during a conference call—in fact, he gets to go to the bathroom most often by himself!_____
- You feel that your husband is usually home during the easier times, like dinner and bedtime or weekend family activities, and seems to miss the more stressful ups and downs of the regular day with the kids._____
- He seems to get more recognition if he stays with the kids, whereas the same is automatically expected of you. He gets kudos if he makes any effort at all._____
- You often feel that he doesn't appreciate all you might go through in a day and he doesn't acknowledge your daily accomplishments, like the details of getting the kids to school and doctor appointments, cleaning the house, and doing the laundry._____

Are you a servant to your feelings of frustration and resentment toward your husband?

◆ **Tips for Becoming a Goddess in Your Relationship with Your Husband** ◆

If your husband is the breadwinner, that typically means he leaves the house every day and has his own world, friends, lunch break, and

solitary trips to the little boys' room. He doesn't understand the world of the stay-at-home mom, as much as he might profess to. It is impossible for him to completely understand. This is a fact. Bringing him closer to understanding is one thing, but you can't expect him to totally get it. Initially, this can be very frustrating. If you allow resentment to fester, it can be a major obstacle to your happiness.

Here are some of our MomsTown tips to deal with the different roles you and your husband play.

- Acceptance gives us freedom. Be aware that your role and your husband's role are inherently different and cannot be compared. They serve unique purposes, but they are of equal importance. Have confidence and know that truth.

- Don't buy into the concept that what he does at work is more important than what you do at home. If you give in to the perception that what you are doing at home is not as important as what your husband does at work, then you are not giving yourself enough credit. Stop that! When your husband comes home and says, "What did you do today?" where do you begin? Maybe you didn't sign off on a huge business merger, accomplish a company project, or get a raise, but you accomplished a million deceptively small yet significant things. In the grand scheme of the success of your relationship and family life you make great strides every day. Believe your role in the home is critical.

- Communicate with him; don't preach. Convey some of the details of your accomplishments and how important you believe they are. We tell moms to communicate their worth as a SAHM to their husband explicitly, if he does not understand. You contribute to his peace of mind, which enables him to concentrate on his job during the day. Your work enables him to do his work. In the long run, the more confident you are about what you do on a daily basis, the more confidence your husband will have in you.

• Involve him in the children's activities. It is also important to form a working relationship with your husband that pulls him into the children's lives, despite his daytime absence. Sometimes we can get so bogged down or resentful of the fact our partner has a life outside the home that we ignore the work of integrating him into the raising of our children. Having a mutually supportive relationship takes work on both ends—you and your husband must make an effort. Be aware of this obstacle and notice it when it crops up.

• Teach him to appreciate your efforts. Naturally, we want to be recognized and acknowledged for what we do at home. This may not come naturally to your husband; he is a man, after all! Sometimes you just have to tell him you need to hear "good job" when you make it through a day with a thousand things to do, or "thank you" when he opens the closet to find his clothes clean and pressed. Explain to him you need the same support and affirmation he expects from and gives to his coworkers at the office.

• Your relationship requires maintenance. Just like a car, your relationship with your husband requires tune-ups and regular care. One of the primary issues in maintaining your relationship with your husband is intimacy. You may be too exhausted with your daily routine, or not confident enough in your own identity, to be enthused about sex. Just as finding yourself takes work, so does intimacy. Take note if you find you're unable to develop a nurturing, exciting sense of intimacy with your husband. We will give you some tips on how to revitalize your chemistry with him later in the book, but for now remember that your relationship will not flourish without effort.

After you have stuck to our philosophy and put in some hard work, your husband will be in awe of you, and you will have more balance in your life and relationships.

The Baby Blues

The Baby Blues happen most often to new moms, but depression can strike any mom. "The Baby Blues" usually refers to the period immediately after giving birth, but sometimes the blues linger as your child grows older. We often think we are not supposed to have the blues. But let's admit it. We do. We do feel blue. You may not know how to explain it. It may seem hard to discuss with anyone else because it's rarely talked about; and, darn it, this is supposed to be the happiest time of your life—you've been blessed with these wonderful children! That's true, but the baby blues strike, and if the symptoms are ignored, it can be serious. If you are feeling funky, have feelings you can't shake, are lethargic and despondent, and you just don't want to get out of the bed in the morning, you must pick up the phone today. Call your doctor. Then call your mom, your sister, your friend, and your husband. You need support and help, and there is nothing wrong with admitting it. In fact, that kind of courage is applauded in MomsTown.

We are here to tell you, it has been clinically proven that there is a hormonal shift in your body that can cause mild to severe depression after you have a baby. New mothers with young babies sometimes experience some form of postpartum depression. Sometimes it will happen directly after you have your baby or will develop in the weeks afterward. For some it can become very severe and create a psychosis. For others, it is a mild depression that may leave you feeling ashamed that you're not happy with your new baby, or perhaps you feel inadequate as a mother.

As your baby grows, you may experience different types of depression. These feelings can be aggravated by sleep deprivation, lack of social interaction with people outside the home, and the absorbing, overwhelming routine of being a mother.

One of our clients called in to our radio show and explained that she didn't even want to say her name because she was so ashamed of the way she felt. She said she knew she should be happy for her new six-month-old baby but just felt isolated, alone, and depressed. Although she loved her baby, she also couldn't shake the blues. She said, "I just know that my baby is the best thing that has ever happened to me, but why do I keep feeling so terrible? I feel alone, alien to my old life, unfamiliar with my new, and just plain strange."

We reassured her that countless moms feel this way. It didn't mean she was any less of a good mother. But even though it's not an uncommon reaction to having a baby, she didn't have to accept depression as her general state of mind. We recommended she call her doctor immediately, as should you if you have any of the same feelings. It is possible to take care of yourself and be an attentive, present, and caring mother.

The Assessment: Are you a servant to the baby blues?

Take a moment and check in with yourself. Do any of the following scenarios sound familiar? Do this exercise like the one above, using 1 to 10 as a measure for how frequently you feel this way.

• Even though you have your children around you, you still feel alone. _____

- You feel down when you begin your day because you feel it is the same old routine again, as in the movie *Groundhog Day*._____
- Your emotional ups and downs are like a roller coaster and you can't figure out why._____
- You feel guilty you don't always appreciate the "luxury" of staying at home with the kids._____
- You feel symptoms of depression that get in the way of appreciating every moment with your kids._____

Review your ratings. Are you a goddess or a servant overall? We cannot emphasize enough that occasional mild depression for moms is normal. Experience it with awareness and know that it is a phase. When you begin feeling the Baby Blues, here are some basic truths to remember.

- Just because you have these feelings, it does not mean you are inadequate.

- You are not a bad, unfit mom.

- These feelings do not mean you do not love your children.

- These feelings are normal, hormonal feelings, but may intensify if you're not being true to your own dreams.

Here's the good news—getting a life can help ward off depression and feelings of unhappiness. It will give you energy, confidence, and a passion for your life. That said, this book is no substitute for professional care. If you or a loved one experiences longer bouts of the blues, seek professional help as soon as possible. This is something we cannot emphasize enough.

Stay at Homework: During your next GAL Diary Duty, record in your diary the details of a depression you might have felt at some point. Allow the memory or the present feeling to flow onto the page. You deserve to have feelings of unhappiness as much as happiness. Admit to yourself that occasional blues are natural. And so is your right to happiness!

Environmental Traps: The SAHM Munchies

What's in your pantry? Is it stuffed with a bunch of those sugary treats that are marketed specifically to moms and kids? These are your enemy—weapons of the Anti-Gal! The Anti-Gal is everything that keeps you from getting it all.

The Assessment: Are you a servant to junk food?

Do any of the following scenarios sound familiar? Do this exercise like the previous one, using a scale from 1 to 10 as a measure of frequency.

- Your pantry is full of packaged, fun-shaped snacks or sugary cereal, chips, crackers, and cookies._____
- You know these foods are bad for you, but you feel that you "deserve" them._____
- You have a bunch of junk food you use to "reward" yourself and your children._____
- You justify having the junk food in your pantry for when you don't have time to fix a healthy snack or dinner._____

Review your ratings. Are you a goddess or a servant overall? If you find you are even a teensy-weensy bit of a servant to junk food, throw that food out today! Starches and sugary foods only make you more hungry and more exhausted in the long run. They are energy-zapping enemies to a Gal. They make your waist wider, your self-confidence shrink, and your energy level plummet. They feed irritability, and this will show when you deal with your children. When your kids eat junk food, they certainly become harder to handle. Grouchy, irritable, and tired, your kids will be tougher to deal with and will develop bad eating habits.

One of our moms, Bonnie, said that after changing her pantry contents, "I realized that whenever the kids got hungry I would reach for a chocolate snack, chips, or junk cereal for them. I had been corralled into buying it at the grocery because my kids had seen all of the commercials for the foods on TV. I gave in and began to notice the kids got whinier in the afternoons and they had trouble sleeping for their nap if they had had too much sugar. When I tossed out all of the snacks, they didn't like the fruit I gave them instead—at first. Now, they don't get as tired or grouchy during the afternoon, and it's worth any initial complaints I get from them. I've begun eating healthier, too, as a result. Now I stick to having a healthy kitchen because it makes my days easier."

Stay at Homework: Take a garbage bag and go through your pantry and kitchen this week. Get everything you know you and your kids should not be eating out of your kitchen. Fill your kitchen with healthy snacks like low-fat granola and fruit. Make these healthier foods readily available so that when you don't have time to fix something to eat, you don't resort to junk food. Do it for yourself and your kids. Bad eating habits are easy to fall back on when you're overbooked, stressed, and not feeling all that great about yourself.

> ♦ Hip Tip: Become a detective. Read the product labels.
> Watch for the amount of saturated fat, trans fats,
> and snacks that are high in calories or sodium. ♦

♦ **Hip Tip: Healthier alternatives to popular snacks.** ♦

Nuts, especially peanuts and almonds. Toss in a few raisins for
a taste of sweetness and a bonus—those little gems pack a lot
of iron.

Popcorn. This is one of our favorite snacks. Make it the old-
fashioned way on the stove or use the microwavable kind.
Remember: use less sodium and butter!

A variety of fresh and dried fruits.

The SAHM Sweats

Let's take a look in your closet. What are you dressing yourself in as
you present yourself to the rest of the world every day?

The Assessment: Are you a servant to sweats or unflattering clothing?

Do any of the following scenarios sound familiar? Do this exercise
like the previous ones, using a scale from 1 to 10 as a measure of
frequency.

- You have a pair of sweatpants you throw on whenever you
  don't feel like getting dressed._____
- You often wear an old outfit you know doesn't flatter you but
  feels safe._____
- Most of your underwear looks like your grandmother's
  drawers._____
- You can't remember the last time you wore something that you
  might have worn *before* you had children._____
- You feel getting dressed is just going through the motions,
  and you rarely get excited about wearing something
  special._____

- You feel depressed when you look into your closet because nothing really fits you anymore (it seems as if all your clothes are either too tight or too baggy)._____
- Everything seems to be the same drab color._____
- You no longer pick outfits based on colors that make you feel good._____
- You don't remember the last time you bought something "special" to wear._____

If your assessment reveals that you lean toward being a servant to sweats or unflattering clothes that don't make you feel like a goddess, then you need to have a wardrobe overhaul! Some of these clothes might have been fine as maternity options, but if you're not pregnant, don't dress as if you are!

You need a wardrobe fit for a Gal or a goddess, not a sweat suit fit for a drab, exhausted SAHM. That's not how you want to be perceived, so don't dress like it. Later in the book we will discuss reinventing your sense of identity, and part of that will be your exterior.

Stay at Homework: Sometime this week, grab a garbage bag and go through your closet.

- Throw out those clothes that don't make you feel good. Get rid of clothes that have stains or holes, and shoes that hurt your feet—no matter how cute they are.

- Go through your underwear and bras, and assess whether or not you have anything that makes you feel sexy.

- Get rid of colors that do not flatter you or make you feel like your authentic self.

• Get rid of anything you haven't worn in the past two years, unless it's that teddy you've been ignoring.

As you weed out your closets, be honest. Do you really like the way these clothes make you feel? If not, good-bye to that old faithful pair of sweats! Good-bye to that muddy-colored, stained shirt that was way too baggy! Don't feel bad about throwing things away. Tell that inner pack rat that Goodwill needs your help. Then drop off those bags of clothes and be done with it!

One of our MomsTown moms, Terra, says of her wardrobe, "Now that I've taken away a lot of the clothes I used to resort to as comfort clothes, usually the baggy, blah-colored pants and shirts, I only have clothes to choose from that fit me or have uplifting colors. I have basically forced myself to dress better by making my comfort clothes less available in the mornings when I start my day. Instead of resorting to my sweatpants and T-shirt in my dresser drawer, I go to the closet, where I have a pair of capris or a skirt and a cute top. My whole persona is different. I don't dread going into the grocery store and standing next to a woman who was at work all day and looks so much more put together than I do. I have my own look now."

◆ Tips for Getting Your Outer Gal Back on Track ◆

We will cover much of your appearance and maintenance of looks and wardrobe later in the program. At this point, though, we would like you to go ahead and take care of what we see as some major details for your new Gal appearance.

• If you have not had a great haircut, color, or highlights within the past eight weeks, pick up the phone and make an appointment.

Don't let anything hold you back, like not knowing exactly what you want—the very act of doing this for yourself is necessary. If you keep telling yourself you can't afford it, go to a discount place or use a salon trainee. The important part is that you do something proactive about your appearance; you don't need to put a dent in your wallet.

• This week, each time you go to your closet to get dressed, look for a color that speaks to you; do not just pick your outfit by default because it is there and comfortable.

• Next time you are in a department store, pharmacy, or mall, stop by the makeup counter and buy a shade of lipstick or lip gloss you've never worn before.

You deserve to look and feel like a real Gal!

Stay at Homework: During your next GAL Diary Duty, take a moment and think back to when you put on clothes that flattered your complexion, figure, and personality. You deserve to look as good as you can—every day. Record a memory you might have of a day or night when you felt beautiful. Maybe it was a first date or a dance. You can have that feeling again.

Your Separate Identity

Trying to find your identity can be challenging when you have been preoccupied with learning how to be a mother. Figuring out what your preferences are and what you are interested in takes commitment. Once you find out who you are and what your passions are, you must stick with developing them.

Answer the following questions in your GAL Diary—honestly. Think long and hard before you answer.

- When you were a little girl, what did you want to be when you grew up?

- What were you good at in high school and college? Was there a particular task that was always allocated to you because it was your specialty?

- Did you have a person you admired whom you wanted to be like? If so, why did you admire them? What qualities did they demonstrate?

- When you were young, was there something you found yourself exceptionally creative with (drawing, writing, singing, dancing, etc.)?

- Make a list of ten things you enjoy doing when you have the time to do them. Nothing is too far out of reach (cooking, taking pictures, hiking, reading, painting, playing the piano, yoga, boxing, biking, writing).

Read over your answers to the above questions. Do you feel a familiar tug inside that you are not doing many of the things that you would like to? The MomsTown program will change that. As soon as you decide who you aspire to be deep down, in the forgotten recesses of yourself, you can work toward allowing those inner desires to become outer results.

Now, for Week 2 of the program, choose one activity you named and plan to do it either by yourself or with the kids. No excuses! If you have to cancel something to fit the activities into your schedule, do it.

WEEK 2 SUMMARY

1. Pick one activity that you feel obligated to do. Say no, even if you don't have another obligation.

2. Remember to repeat your GAL Mantra when you feel guilt or fear. Take note of how often you feel guilt and fear and when your actions are motivated by these feelings.

3. Remember to go over the tips for dealing with the hubby when you feel frustrated and underappreciated.

4. Remember that the blues or down feelings you might have are natural, but will soon begin to become less frequent as you get a life.

5. Clean out your pantry and kitchen: Throw away any junk food, starches, and sugary snacks.

6. Evaluate your everyday wardrobe. Abandon the sweats and unflattering styles or colors. Save gym clothes for the gym.

7. Make your haircut appointment.

8. Dress in colors that make you feel vibrant and beautiful.

9. Make an "Anti-Clutter" list and keep adding to it as you think of new things.

10. Do a fun activity, with or without the kids, that you have not done in the past two months.

WEEK 3: GET ORGANIZED: GET INTO THE FLOW

It's time to get organized. Organization is your magic key to opening up all sorts of possibilities for yourself. The more organized you are, the more you can do. Most of the stress SAHMs feel can be traced to disorganization. We often hear from our clients who come to this part of the program that perhaps they just aren't "detail people," that there aren't enough hours in the day, or that they aren't particularly good at organization. Even if you don't consider yourself organized, a little attention and work in the beginning of your day and throughout can make a world of difference.

We've all been in Flow Motion even though we may not have known it at the time. Flow Motion is that moment when you are moving seamlessly from one thing to another, getting things done and feeling like a goddess, not a servant. This week we are going to show you ways to get into Flow Motion, be more organized, efficient, and confident about your schedule and sense of accomplishment. Disorganization puts you into turbid waters. The goal for the MomsTown mom is to move out of the muddy waters of piles of paper in the kitchen, colliding schedules, overflowing closets, and smashed crackers in the car seats. When you are in Flow Motion, your day runs fluidly, leaving you free to explore the open waters of your potential.

At MomsTown we know that anyone can be well organized. Organization is a state of mind. We would like you to repeat to yourself, right now,

I am an organized person.

We ask that you repeat that to yourself when you feel you have too much to do in a day or forget something you feel you should have remembered. If your mind feels capable of being organized, it's a lot easier to get there. On the MomsTown program, we tell all of our moms that organization is a beautiful thing. But make no mistake, organization takes work. Let's get started.

THE GAL ORGANIZER

This week, your first task is to get an organizer, portable calendar, or Palm Pilot. Get something that works for you. If you already have an organizer, this is a good time to evaluate whether or not you are using your organizer to its fullest potential, or if it has features that meet all of your needs. If you are not good with gadgets and feel crazy when you try to figure out how your cell phone voice mail works, get a paper organizer. If you enjoy learning about technology and a Palm Pilot sounds exciting to you, then go for it. If you decide on a paper organizer, make sure of the following:

1 There is enough room on the separate day sections to write a good-size list for that particular day (up to twelve tasks).

2 It has a section where you can view a whole month at a time.

3 There is a zipper or snap, in case you have loose papers to keep.

4 It is not too big to fit into your purse (unless you have an unusually tiny purse).

5 It has a small pad for grocery lists. This pad will also be for your "Running Task" list (more on this to come).

6 There is room for a small pen inside, so that not having a pen won't be an excuse for forgetting to write something down. If you can't find one with a pen, clip your own inside.

7 There is room for something personal, such as pictures of the kids, a favorite quote, or a picture of you at your happiest moment.

Your organizer should be uplifting and full of inspiration. It should give you the feeling that you are "on purpose" with your life.

THE HOT IRON TASK

Now that you have a personal organizer, we would like to add another step to your morning routine. We moms have long had so many irons in the fire, it's hard to figure out what to do first. At MomsTown, we start each day (after making the bed) by choosing what the "Hot Iron" for that day will be. The Hot Iron is what you will focus on *and* accomplish that day, no matter what. Often we try to do too much as moms and can fall into the trap of trying to do five things at once and not getting any of them finished. At MomsTown, we have discovered that if you focus on one thing each day you can

- have a sense of accomplishment because you have completed the Hot Iron task for the day.

- begin the morning with the Hot Iron task as priority #1. Then go down the list and number other tasks you'd *like* to get done that day in order of their priority.

- tackle other tasks after you complete the Hot Iron task.

- talk to your husband when he comes home without being overwhelmed by the fifty things you meant to do. You can always refer to the Hot Iron task.

For SAHMs, stress can come from feeling as if we don't have anything tangible to show for all our work during the day. Choosing a task, focusing on it, and moving on to the next task allows you to feel organized right off the bat in the morning. We do not want you to do only one thing a day: Not only would your life grind to a halt, but your life would be nearly impossible. We ask only that you focus on one thing per day to take priority above the rest.

The Hot Iron task should be specific. Examples include paying the bills, cleaning the kitchen, going to the grocery store, going to the bank, or cleaning out a closet.

As soon as you are finished making your bed in the morning, go to your daily schedule and choose what your Hot Iron for the day will be.

Write that on your daily calendar and begin your list there. Let all of your other tasks line up after the Hot Iron.

BE LOYAL TO YOUR SCHEDULE

Yes, this seems like an obvious point, but it is very important: Be loyal to your schedule. It takes discipline and focus to stick to one's schedule. You must regard your schedule with respect and honor. Below are some tips on how to think of your schedule.

- Treat your SAHM commitments as if they were professional commitments. Give commitments on your schedule the same attention that you would in a career-oriented environment. Examples:

  Your workout time = an important company meeting
  The Hot Iron = a company project with an immediate deadline

- As we said above, and we can't say enough, check your schedule in the morning when choosing your Hot Iron and writing your list.

- Check off items as you accomplish them on your schedule. This leads to a sense of progress and ensures that you keep referring to your schedule.

- Don't overschedule and make yourself crazy! Keep more than enough time between appointments or engagements so you don't get stressed out if one of the kids has an accident with his juice in the car or you forget his stuffed animal at the library and have to retrace your steps. Make sure your schedule allows for the unpredictable life of a mom.

• Schedule exercise appointments.

• Schedule personal time.

One of our moms, Rhonda, says of her schedule, "My schedule is my friend. It is there to keep me going and focused when I feel that I have a trillion things to do. I absolutely love checking things off my schedule. It makes me feel like I'm making progress in my day." Schedules are our allies. Make sure you treat them that way by sticking to your list and allowing the schedule to help you.

Running Task List

This is something we use all of the time. It is one of the essential parts of the GAL Organizer. In your organizer you should have a Running Task list. Your Running Task list is basically your to-do list. As you think of things, this is where you write them down if you can't fit them in your schedule today or tomorrow but need to remember them. This is where you scribble something you don't want to forget and need to follow up with. We will incorporate using this Running Task list in your daily routine later in this chapter.

One of the keys to organization is figuring out what types of schedules work for you and your personal style. Some of our moms are very strategic about their weekly schedule. One mom, Candy, says of hers, "I clean one thing each day. Monday=Kitchen Overhaul; Tuesday=Bathrooms; Wednesday=Laundry; Thursday=Dusting; Friday=Floors. This works well. I may not get to each chore each day, but at least I know where I stand and it is a little more difficult to become so overwhelmed with the cleaning. I usually do these chores before my daughter wakes up, or finish them while she is enjoying her Cheerios in the high chair."

Are you someone who likes to do all of your cleaning in one day or the whole week? Evaluate what type of schedule you are comfortable with and stick to it.

Mastering the Quarter Hour

Fifteen minutes may not seem like a lot of time to most people, but to a mom every fifteen counts. You would be surprised what you can get done in a quarter hour. As John F. Kennedy said, "We must use time as a tool and not a crutch." The MomsTown philosophy is to use every fifteen minutes to your advantage—and to make fifteen minutes available to yourself even when you don't think you have it. Making the quarter hour a tool is one of the best ways to keep yourself organized and on schedule. We have a few tips to show you how to use the quarter hour to your advantage.

Set your alarm clock fifteen minutes back in the mornings. If you and your husband typically get up at 6 A.M., set it for 5:45 and allow yourself some time alone to get organized and ready for the day. How you start your day is how you will run your day. If you are awake and composed instead of running late and harried, you will have a better day.

Do fifteen minutes of de-cluttering at a time. You may feel that some of your de-cluttering projects are just too overwhelming to start immediately. If you take a spare fifteen minutes between driving your daughter to ballet lessons and finishing a phone call to de-clutter your kitchen table, counter, or home office desk, it will make you feel a lot more effective and a lot less behind. De-cluttering as you go can make your day more organized all around. Things won't pile up and you'll be ahead of the game when it's time to clean.

Schedule your calendar in fifteen-minute increments. We've talked about being loyal to your schedule. Make appointments with yourself and keep them. The appointments may be as simple as calling the school auction committee or making a dentist appointment. Take them seriously by scheduling them for yourself and you won't have difficulty forgetting things as often.

If you are feeling distracted or disorganized, take fifteen minutes to clean out your car or purse. These two places get the most disorganized when we are busy. Cleaning them out can make you feel a lot more on top of things.

Take fifteen minutes to go over your schedule, calendar, and task list. What have you done or not done? Check off things you've done and do a quick prioritizing of things you should be doing. You should do this in the morning, but as moms, we know that things change during the day and an item on our list may become more important than it was initially.

Take fifteen minutes to decide what you're having for dinner and get a recipe. Do you feel you never have enough time to decide what is for dinner until a half hour before it's time to eat? When you do decide, do you tend to make that "fallback dish" you resort to when you don't know what else to make? Take fifteen minutes to go online to MomsTown.com or another Web site such as epicurious.com and get a new, interesting recipe. Print it out or copy it down, and you've got a grocery list for yourself and a new entrée to add to the dinner selection.

As you can see from our tips, we've found you can get tasks done in the quarter hour that can help shape your accomplishments of the day and get you organized. Always know that you can get something finished in fifteen minutes that may make your day. It is possible. Take advantage of the quarter hour and try our tips out this week. You don't have to do them all at once. Try to do one a day and see how they help you stay on task and organized!

THE HOME OFFICE

Even if you don't have a room dedicated to a home office, it is important to have an area that has a desk and some file cabinets or shelves. If you can't afford to buy a desk at this time, put a makeshift one together with a table. The point of having a home office is to designate a place where your work, bills, and paperwork will be organized. Otherwise, you will find yourself leaving papers around the house, using the kitchen counter or dining-room table for bills and mail, and even worse, losing important papers, missing bill due dates, and feeling disorganized. This week, if you don't have a home office, establish one in a corner of a room, maybe the guest room or the living room. Avoid choosing the bedroom. When you're ready for bed, you need to distance yourself from the business of the home office. Bedtime should be a peaceful time with your husband (we will get to that later in the book). If you already have a home office, take this week to organize it.

Once you have established your home office, treat it like a real office. Give it the respect it deserves.

Your home office should be your place, away from where the kids play. One of our MomsTown members, Edna, says of her home office, "When I sit down to my computer, I feel as if I have a purpose separate from my kids, because I am in some way connecting with the outside world, whether it be looking over a bank statement or ordering books from Amazon." Once she set up her office and took advantage of it, Edna's home office became her refuge.

Below are some tips for keeping your home office tidy and efficient.

- Keep the papers in files, either in file cabinets or accordion folders.

- Throw away junk mail the second it hits your hands. Tear up solicitations for credit cards and the like.

- Keep things filed in their correct places, rather than littering the top of the desk or table.

- Make labels for things you find don't fit in the typical files of bills, receipts, etc. For example, you may have baby gear instruction manuals out the wazoo, or medical and insurance papers that flood your home after your baby is born. Make a folder for each of the different companies you deal with.

- Get an in-box and an out-box so you can keep current projects organized rather than leaving them scattered on the desk.

- Keep a nice plant on or near your desk. This will help you feel it is a pleasant place to spend time.

Figure out ways to organize your office that work for you. One of our moms, Betty, has worked out methods that make her feel efficient and organized. "My mail goes straight from the mailbox to be filed, placed in a bill-payment cubby, or tossed. I have a bill-payment cubby—actually it's just a thin notebook file with the names of each bill we get from month to month on each divider. New bills get placed in the file pocket straight from the mailbox and old ones are filed in a separate file folder as soon as they are paid." Certain methods will work for you and others won't. Experiment with different mail-sorting systems until you find a technique that is ideal for your habits and schedule.

Don't Let Paperwork Take Over Your Life

Keeping important papers is one thing, but we can easily get confused about what is important and what is not when we are not paying attention to it on a regular basis.

This week go through your home office and adhere to the following rules:

• Clothing receipts: for the length of the return policy.

• Credit card slips: monthly until the statement arrives and you use receipts to match purchases. Then you can toss them.

• ATM receipts: record on your check registry and then toss them.

Keep receipts for these items for as long as you own the related item:

• Automobile records
• Furniture
• Appliances
• Investments (records of purchases and sales)
• Mortgage(s)
• Property bills
• Household appraisals

Keep these for five years or more:

- Medical and tax documents
- Receipts for home improvements
- Bank statements
- Credit card statements
- Check registers

Keep these forever:

- Vital records: birth certificates, social security cards and records
- Marriage certificates
- Divorce papers
- Wills

Cut the cord and toss these:

- Old coupons: Do these really save you money? Be honest.

- Old greeting cards: unless they are very, very special.

- Old invitations: There are exceptions (your wedding), but most can be tossed (your neighbor's cocktail party).

- Expired insurance policies: Don't worry!

- Magazines over two months old: Don't let these lie around your house and clutter your coffee table. If you like to have them in your bathroom, don't keep more than two.

- Mail-order catalogs over a month old: You can always go online.

- Tourist brochures from old vacations: Chances are you have pictures, which are much better.

- Bad photos: Forget the rule that says you should keep every photo. Toss 'em, especially if you don't look your best.

- Charity solicitations you don't give to: These charities are not benefiting from your keeping the material.

Use discipline to throw away unnecessary clutter and paperwork. This week, go through your paperwork and follow the above guidelines. Be strict! Remember, your peace of mind is more important than keeping excess clutter.

After one of our moms, Betsy, attacked the piles of paper on her desk and drawers, she reported: "I don't know why I always tortured myself by keeping every single greeting card I got. I had hundreds, and they were taking over my paper storage areas. I think I felt rude throwing them away, like they were sentimental relics. Now I realize that I can just let go, and it feels so much better."

THE NIGHT BEFORE

At MomsTown we like to wake up early and know we're starting fresh, rather than having to finish or clean up after projects that were left halfway done the night before. If you are cleaning up from the night before, you are starting your day behind. Not only are you behind in your schedule, but you are also behind mentally. Taking care of a mess on the kitchen table or a paperwork project you began the night before—instead of dealing with your Hot Iron task first thing—can be draining and disheartening. That's why we ask that during this third week you form the habit of going through the Night Before checklist.

- Wipe kitchen counter and table surfaces clean with disinfectant.

- Gather loose papers and projects and file them in the home office so you will have a smooth, clutter-free surface to begin the next day. Use your in-box or out-box to put your current project in if it is too involved to tackle in one day.

- Put any dirty clothes and towels in the laundry bin.

- Make sure all of the dishes have been washed and there are none left in the sink. Wash them or put them in the dishwasher. If your dishwasher is full, run it right before you go to bed—it feels great to wake up to a full set of clean dishes.

- Go over your schedule checklist on your calendar and move anything you might have not gotten done to tomorrow's list. Go over your Running Task list and see if anything from that can be added to your next-day schedule.

- If you have a lot on your mind, grab your diary and make an entry. Getting concerns onto the page can help you sleep better.

If you learn to run through this checklist in your mind before going to bed at night, we promise you will sleep better, wake up feeling refreshed, and have a more productive morning and following day. Even if you're tired, do it. In the long run you will save energy by cleaning up after yourself before the sun rises again.

One of our MomsTown members, Amy, says of her Night Before checklist, "Even if I am exhausted from the day, getting the kids to bed and cooking dinner, I still make myself do the Night Before list. It just makes such a difference when I wake up in the morning. I can immediately feel organized and ready for the day. I can't remember a night when I haven't done the list since beginning the program—I'm hooked."

Another MomsTown member, Bernice, remembers to check her schedule, but is forgiving if something comes up with the kids. "Before I go to bed each night, I look at my calendar and make a tentative list of what needs to be accomplished the next day. That way, my days take some sort of shape while not being overly restrictive. If my daughter doesn't nap on schedule or is fussy, I'm not too scheduled to handle it." This is a good way to handle our schedules. The night before can feel overwhelming when we take a look at all of the things we have to do, but remember, as we said earlier in this chapter, your life is unpredictable, and having a firm but not overly restrictive schedule will make you less stressed.

GET HELP FROM YOUR KIDS

You need help with some of the maintenance of running your household and staying organized. If your kids are young, help them establish habits that will teach organization and help you in the process. Here are some strategies for bringing your kids into the fold. Some apply to older kids, and some apply to all ages. Use your discretion as to which are appropriate for your brood.

Pick your battles to win the war. Let's forget what your kids do to clutter the whole house and their bedrooms for a moment and focus. Begin bringing them into the organization routine by choosing one room they're responsible for picking up. For most people, it is the living room or den, because that is where the family relaxes together. For others, it may be the kitchen. You won't get any saner by trying to get them to keep every inch of the house in order all of the time, so begin with your chosen room and tell them to help you keep that neat. One of our moms, Deena, says, "I found that if I tried to get them to do everything I wanted immediately, it just wore me out and they became more burned out about helping. Concentrating on one thing at a time has helped my stress level, their productivity with chores, and our relationships."

Charge them when they keep leaving their clothes and toys in the chosen room. This is a tip you can use if you have older kids. Younger children need to be taught responsibility with positive reinforcement. After you've chosen your room and put your foot down, charge them twenty-five cents every time they leave something in that room. If they have an allowance, take it out of that. You can make a little charge list for the refrigerator and hang it there with a magnet, keeping a tally. One of our moms, Dolly, began doing this and found, "Once my daughter realized money was being taken out of her prospective shopping budget, she changed her tune very quickly."

Use baskets, bins, or trunks in various rooms to keep order. Have a designated place to put away any clothing that's lying around on the floor, bed, or other parts of the house. This way, it isn't complicated to tidy up. You can integrate a trunk into your decorating scheme and just open the top and put toys in at clean-up time. It's much easier than lugging all of the toys back and forth from the bedroom or playroom. Toys can be challenging, since they seem to clutter every corner of your house.

One of our moms, Trina, shared her toy organizational methods. "I absolutely love those three-drawer clear plastic organizers and use those to keep the girls' toys in. The best rule of organizing is to learn what to keep and what to toss out. Happy Meal toys, toys with missing parts, and/or ones that don't work anymore don't stick around my house for very long. I also keep a minimal amount of toys downstairs and the rest of my daughters' toys are kept upstairs in their room—in the same three-drawer organizers. I recycle toys every month or so and bring new toys downstairs, putting others away. I go through and weed out throwaways and take 'old' toys upstairs. All of my daughters' hardcover books have been laminated and they are kept in a magazine rack. My youngest likes to chew on book covers and used to rip pages before I decided to laminate all of their books. I recycle their books the same way I do their toys, but more often because they love to read."

Pick a Hot Iron for your kids. Depending on their ages and your determination as to what they can and cannot do, try to prioritize for them. Pick what they must concentrate on and ask that it be accomplished in a specific period of time.

Concentrate on their effort, not their results. This is important especially if they are young. If they are making a tremendous effort to pick up their blocks, to feed the cat, or to clean up their room, but they don't do the job perfectly, praise them! Don't criticize. They are putting the energy toward learning to do chores. By the time they are old enough and able, they will be in the habit of understanding that their effort is greatly appreciated. "When I concentrate on how well my child is doing as far as focusing on the task at hand, rather than critiquing him, he enjoys the praise so much. It has made him want to do more to please me," Jonnie, MomsTown member, says.

Make a chore calendar. This one can be handled according to the ages of your kids. Have chores listed by day on a calendar on the fridge. Make sure to list not only the daily ones, like making the bed, setting the table, emptying the dishwasher, and picking up their toys, but also the weekly ones, like helping to vacuum, mowing the lawn, etc. Get them in the habit of referring to their list and have them check off the chores they do as they do them, even if you have to help them because they cannot read yet. By assigning them specific chores and things they are good at, you make it easier for yourself in the long run. One of our moms, Cathy, did this and got great results. "My children are responsible for emptying wastepaper baskets and taking out the garbage, as well as clearing the table and cleaning up after themselves. This helps keep the house in order. My younger daughter is also great at cleaning bathrooms."

One of the focuses of this week should be to help integrate good habits of organization into your kids' behavior patterns. Just getting them into the routine of doing chores and helping with the overall cleanliness of the house is a huge start.

The Assessment: Are you a servant to clutter in your home?

Just like the assessments we did in Week 2, we are going to assess where you stand with your clutter factor.

Do any of the following scenarios sound familiar? Do this exercise like the ones above, using a scale from 1 to 10 as a measure of frequency.

- Your home is a trap for odds and ends, old and unused toys and impulse buys, and a mishmash of items that you don't remember the origin of. _____
- You often cannot find items like scissors, tools, and needles when you need them. _____
- When you enter the garage, attic, or certain closets, you try to exit as soon as possible because the clutter makes you feel uncomfortable. _____
- You admire others' homes and sparse, clean surfaces. You find yourself wishing yours could be as organized. _____
- You feel so overwhelmed by your clutter that you have no

idea where to start and are almost convinced organization is impossible. _____

Are you a servant to clutter and disorganization? By the time we are done with you, you'll be a goddess, and the clutter will be history!

MAKE YOUR ANTI-CLUTTER LIST

Take a moment, grab your diary, and make a list of all of the areas in your home you would like to be better organized. Below is a sample Anti-Clutter list—no area can be too small. In fact, the tighter the focus, the better. On your list, be specific. Avoid grouping things, like "all closets" or "the living room." There should be at least ten areas on your list.

Spice rack
Living room bookcase
Bedroom closet
Hall closet
Bathroom cabinets
Kitchen cupboard
Underwear drawer
Kids' wardrobe

Leave room at the end of the list for any additions you might have now that you are on the lookout.

Stay at Homework: This week, choose one task from the clutter list that you just made and tackle it. You can choose a small or large task, depending on your schedule. Write this task on your daily schedule and allow yourself a fair amount of time to do it. Treat it like a work or professional appointment and don't skip it! We will continue choosing a task from the Anti-Clutter list each week of the program. During a hectic week, it can be as simple as a drawer in your kitchen. Other weeks, you can pick big projects, like your closets.

Just as you weeded out all of those things in your closet that don't make you feel like the dynamic, spectacular person you really are, you must do the same with your possessions, your decor, and the general state of your home. Remember, your home is the place where you raise your children, live your life, and in some cases, work. It should be a place that makes you feel good when you are there. Clutter interferes with clarity and confidence, and stands in the way of other work. You never feel the best you can feel when you have a bunch of old, unused objects cluttering your personal space. Having kids is not an excuse not to make your home exactly how you like it. If you are happy in your home, your children will be, too.

As you pick up your Anti-Clutter list and get ready to tackle it, remember the following things:

- Recognize that you are the queen of your home. Your attitude, outlook, and confidence are conveyed by the place you make for yourself and your family.

- Assess where you are now, and look for things that do not fit into your vision of yourself.

Are you a servant to your circumstances, many of which you have unwittingly created, or are you a goddess who creates your life the way you want it? The choice is up to you.

◆ Anti-Clutter Tips ◆

Here are a few tips to help you begin your Anti-Clutter list. Sometimes we simply need to give ourselves permission to throw something away. Most of these tips are obvious, but everyone needs reminders as they part with personal clutter.

Get rid of:

- Old gifts that you've kept only to be polite
- Broken appliances that have been left unrepaired for more than two months
- Old batteries
- Any cleaning supplies, sunscreen, or toiletries you have not used in a year
- Gift boxes, wrinkled tissue paper, and old gift bags
- Rusted appliances and tools
- Broken furniture left unrepaired for a year

Enforce these rules, despite any attachment you might have, as you go through your clutter. Remember, you will be relieved when it is out of your house and your mind. As of right now, the clutter serves only to bog you down and is keeping you from being happy in your own home. You will feel so much better after you begin tackling your Anti-Clutter list.

One of our moms, Frances, told us after she had tackled only two items on her Anti-Clutter list, "I feel like a new woman! Just using your simple tips and taking it step by step has made me do a lot of cleaning that I had been putting off for so long. I realized how much better I begin to feel in my home once I didn't allow so many unnecessary items to litter the corners, closets, and living room. I actually feel lighter in my own home now. Before, I would think of everything I needed to clean out and would get overwhelmed. Now I realize just taking one thing at a time makes a huge difference."

Is Your Home Equipped for Organization?

Do you have things set up so that they are most convenient for you to be able to keep things neat? This would mean having specific places for things, like bins for toys, not just in the closet; or racks for shoes, rather than just putting them in a heap at the bottom of the closet. If you don't have specifically designated places for things, you will always be unorganized.

This week, take time to purchase the following if you do not have them:

• Laundry bins for every bedroom. You can have your main basket that you take around to the bins to fill up when it's time to do laundry.

• Toy bins. One trick is to put away half of the toys in a closet or basement every other week and rotate them. That way you have fewer toys to put away.

• Bins in the garage for everything from tools to baseball bats and gloves.

• In your closets you may want to consider stacking plastic drawers for hats, scarves, mittens, etc.; and plastic containers for out-of-season clothing, sewing materials, toiletries, batteries, cleaning supplies, etc.

Now that you are on your way to becoming organized, we are ready to tackle the rest of the MomsTown program. We will build on these organizational lessons and tools. When you've learned to keep a firm schedule, prioritize, and de-clutter your home, you are capable of doing so much more. Remind yourself as often as you need to that you *are* an organized person!

WEEK 3 SUMMARY

1. Organizer: Get your GAL Organizer and start using it this week.

2. Hot Iron: Pick your Hot Iron immediately after making your bed. Pick a Hot Iron every day this week.

3. Schedule: How many days did you stick to your schedule this week? Make sure you check items off as you accomplish them.

4. Home office: Set up your office, take care of it, organize it, and choose a decoration or potted plant for it. Adhere to the MomsTown rules when sorting papers. Go through those stacks of old papers and be tough on yourself.

5. Night Before: Follow the checklist and stick to it every night from now on out.

6. Get help: Enlist your kids in organizational tasks. As soon as they can talk and walk, start very young children on a few basic chores, and remember: It's the effort, not the results, that counts.

7. Anti-Clutter: Make your list and choose one item this week to tackle.

WEEK 4: GETTING A LIFE AND A BODY ATTITUDE TO MATCH

"Fitness is not an event—it's a lifestyle." This is a MomsTown maxim.

Getting your body back is part of the foundation of our program. In our experience with moms, we have found that sticking to workouts and a healthier diet changes not only your exterior but also your interior. Once moms start to work out regularly, their lives begin to fall into place. We guarantee you, if you make the effort to stick to this program and honor your commitment to working out, you will feel a difference almost immediately.

At MomsTown we believe it is difficult to live your life to its fullest if you are not exercising and eating well. If you are not exercising regularly, your blood is not circulating at its peak, your heart is not gaining in strength, your bones are weakening, flexibility and mobility are limited, and you are missing out on the mood-enhancing benefits of a good sweat. Working out and improving your physical image is one cornerstone to getting a life.

Exercise is good for the body, mind, emotions, and soul. Scheduling time for fitness sessions and healthy food will boost your self-image, your energy level, confidence, attitude, and sex life. It is a good habit to exercise on a regular if not daily basis. After a couple of weeks you will miss a skipped exercise session. Your body and mind will crave your workout routine. By the end of the program you will look better in your clothes and feel better about your body. Plus, when you put your workouts high on your list of priorities, you set a great example for your kids. As one of our moms, Paula, found out, "My workout time is sacred, and my kids know it. I alternate between doing exercise videos and using the NordicTrack in the basement; it's important for my children to see me work out because it sets a good example. I want them to know that it's critical to take care of their health. If they don't take care of themselves, they won't be able to take care of anyone else."

This week we are going to concentrate on getting you started on your new body attitude and healthy lifestyle choices. As Paula has discovered, if you don't take care of yourself, you won't be able to take care of anyone else.

The BABS Syndrome

We've all had that moment when we're standing in front of the mirror naked, and we wonder what happened to our reflection. We examine every flaw, bulge, and sag. We long to get our youthful figure back, or we long to have a figure that we can be proud of at the pool. That's why we're going to help you conquer BABS, the boobs, abs, and butt syndrome. These are the three danger zones. We know that when you start to lift your butt, you'll lift your spirits! Let's take a moment to pinpoint what part of the BABS syndrome you are most affected by—your boobs, abs, or butt?

Stay at Homework: Take a moment and make a list in your GAL Diary. What areas of your body would you like to improve?

Get Over Your "Big Buts"

The MomsTown program takes a no-excuses approach to all the issues moms face, including health. There is no excuse for not exercising, and there is no excuse for not eating properly. Trust us, we've heard them all, and we've used them all—no time, no energy, weight has always been an issue, etc. All the excuses moms can muster for not getting fit, we've heard. The one that irks us the most is when women blame their weight issues on pregnancy. Pregnancy makes babies; it doesn't make you fat.

Stay at Homework: Grab your GAL Diary and make a list of all of the excuses you've been using for why you don't look and feel the way you want to. We'll get you started with some of the ones we hear from mothers.

You don't have enough time.
After taking care of the kids and the household, you don't have
    enough energy.
You don't know how to use the machines at the gym.
You don't like to sweat.
You just don't feel motivated.
You think you're coming down with something, so you better
    not push it.
The kids aren't going to want to go to the gym.

Read over your excuses and be honest with yourself. There is no excuse for not giving yourself time to get your body in shape. We're here to tell you, there are a million reasons to get your body in shape. The simplest way to put it is this: Working out is something you must do for yourself.

◆ Hip Tip: Consider working out as the "no-choice" activity of the day. Just as you have no choice but to get out of bed in the morning, you have no choice but to work out. Period. ◆

WHAT'S YOUR BODY ATTITUDE?

Body Attitude is a MomsTown term that refers to the attitude you have about exercise. Your attitude about your exercise regimen spreads to your physical appearance. At MomsTown we concentrate on your Body Attitude and forget all other classifications you may feel you are saddled with. We believe there is a direct link between your Body Attitude and your life outlook. If you work out regularly, you'll have a better attitude and outlook; if you don't, the opposite will happen.

This will be the only time in this book you ever read this, but . . . forget fruit! The body-shape kind, we mean. You are not an apple or a pear. We've had moms say to us, "I found out when I did an exercise program that I am a pear. I guess I'll always be that shape." Forget all of those things you've heard that make you feel you're stuck with the way your body is now. At MomsTown, we don't believe in labeling your shape. Classifying your body implies it cannot change. It's true your body may tend to get a little out of shape in one area faster than another, but ultimately you are in control. When you admit that you can make a difference—that you are not a slave to your genetics—then you have taken the first step toward fitness. Your attitude and your re-lationship with a healthy lifestyle help determine your body shape. Any natural tendencies your body might have to being pearlike, big-boned, or prone to heaviness is no excuse for not getting off the couch, eating properly, and taking responsibility for your own Body Attitude.

At MomsTown, there are exercise GAL Mantras we have our moms say while working out or anytime they feel a bit sluggish and don't really want to go work out:

- I can change my body with the right choices and commitment.

- I deserve to feel healthy.

- Feeling healthy will make me more mentally healthy.

- My body can be as good as I want it to with dedication and hard work.

- The only thing limiting my body potential is myself.

- I deserve to have a body that is as wonderful as I am on the inside.

We ask moms to remember at least two of these mantras when they begin resorting to their old attitudes about working out. Remember, it's all about attitude. You can control your attitude and you can change your attitude. First, let's find out what your Body Attitude is.

If you have a depressed, unadventurous attitude, that is reflected in your body. If you are overweight and don't feel comfortable in your clothes, your inner discontent and lack of motivation spread to your outer Body Attitude. Take a look at the classifications below and see which one suits you. Take the following quiz.

1. Your workout habits and history are most often
   a. making excuses and dreading the exertion of sweating and working out.

    b. beginning a workout plan, doing it for a week or two, and then abandoning it.

    c. finding one exercise activity that feels comfortable and obsessively doing it.

2. When planning vacations or weekends for your family, you

    a. gravitate toward recreational activities that require no physical effort or discomfort.

    b. plan vacations that have a lot of physical recreational activity options, like outdoor hiking, swimming, or biking, and then spend the whole time with your family watching TV and going out to eat.

    c. seek out family activities that require physical activity and athletic learning opportunities.

3. When you think about identifying your personality in relation to sports, gyms, or exercise, you

    a. gravitate toward recreational activities that require no physical effort or discomfort and think of yourself as "not very athletic."

    b. guiltily remember the pile of exercise equipment in the garage or spare bedroom gathering dust. You sometimes consider yourself a jack-of-all-sportlike-trades but a master of none.

    c. are proud of your devotion to exercise and consider it something you can't live without.

4. When you dress in the mornings just to do things around the house, you immediately reach for:

    a. the baggiest, most comfortable, casual outfit that doesn't reveal your figure, regardless of color or style.

    b. clothes you like but that no longer fit you. You keep these clothes in hopes of fitting into them again as soon as you go on your new diet or exercise regimen.

   c. your favorite colored tank top that flatters your tummy and a skirt.

5. When asked by a friend if you want to go to the neighborhood Mexican restaurant during your designated workout time, you usually

   a. choose cheese dip, of course!

   b. note that you didn't eat Mexican for a whole month because you were on a diet, but now that you messed up your diet the night before, what the heck—tacos, here you come!

   c. tell your friend you'll meet her for a margarita later in the week, but for now, your spinning class is calling.

6. When you get three quarters of the way through your workout and you start to feel tired and sweaty, you

   a. don't know how that feels because you don't like sweat.

   b. tell yourself you've done a great job, and now it's time for a snack.

   c. push yourself harder to get finished and consider adding another fifteen minutes to your workout.

Look back over your answers and add them up. For each *a* answer, score 1 point; for each *b*, 2 points; and for each *c*, 3 points. Add up your total.

6–9 points: Unchallenged Body Attitude

10–14 points: Drifter Body Attitude

14–18 points: Vigorous Body Attitude

The Unchallenged Body Attitude

If you have this attitude, you must begin to take baby steps. We promise that once you begin, you will be much happier for it. Your energy, confidence, and passion will increase, and you will understand inherently why exercise is so important.

Take some time today to memorize the exercise GAL Mantras. Later this week, you will choose from among some specific programs, but the main thing you must do now is commit to a program of at least three days a week.

The Drifter Body Attitude

If you have this attitude, you must work on focusing on your goals. You must learn to be devoted to the regularity and routine of a workout. This commitment will pay off in huge dividends, not just physically but mentally as well. The confidence you will gain from sticking to a routine and reaching a goal will be rewarding.

The exercise GAL Mantras we would like you to repeat are:

• I can change my body with commitment.

• My body can be as good as I want it to with dedication and hard work.

• Committing to an exercise schedule is really a commitment to my new life.

The Vigorous Body Attitude

If you have this attitude, you may need to work on varying your routine if you find yourself sticking to only one activity. Perhaps you love running and do only that. You must take that devotion and drive and put it toward different types of exercise: strength training, interval sprints, and other variations on what you are comfortable doing. There is always a new mountain to climb! If you vary your exercise routine, you will constantly be challenging your body. To make your body the fittest it can be and to make your workouts as fulfilling and exciting as they can be, it is important to explore other types of exercise.

If you have a vigorous Body Attitude, we would like you to work on varying your routine. Your exercise GAL Mantras are:

◆ I can change my body by being unafraid of a new challenge.

◆ The only thing limiting my body potential is my comfort zone.

◆ Tips for a Successful Exercise Routine ◆

We have some tips on how we make it through the week and make sure we put our time in at the gym or outdoors for regular, fun workouts. If you keep these tips in mind, it will make your commitment to your body and your workout schedule much easier.

- **Follow the GAL Exercise Rules.** This week, we would like you to do the following regardless of what program you choose (we will provide program suggestions later in this chapter):

  Do a workout three days a week for at least 30 minutes a day. More time is fine, less is not.

  At the beginning of each week, on Sunday, schedule your workouts in your organizer.

  Your workouts are your lifeline and cannot be negotiated or changed.

Challenge yourself during your workout. Strive to sweat! Sweating is actually sexy and healthy; it releases toxins and it feels great.

Keep a change of clothing in your trunk (deodorant, shoes, workout clothes) so you can work out at any time.

* **Exercise consistently and at the same frequency.** You must stick to regular, consistent workouts. Whether these are spinning, yoga, Pilates, aerobics, treadmill, free weights, running, biking, or walking outside, there must be a respected, sacred commitment to it on your schedule. As we said in the last chapter, your schedule should receive the same respect that you would give a professional work schedule. Your workout time is not flexible, movable, or "penciled in" on your calendar. It is there and present, in pen, and has the same importance as your husband's board meeting or your son's Little League game. Why? Because it keeps you on track, it keeps your energy up, and you are a better mother when you like the way you look and feel.

  We work out at five in the morning three times a week. The extra effort of waking up early is worth it to get our workout in. Making that time for ourselves is as important as anything else we do. The GAL Exercise Rules will help you stay consistent.

  One of our moms, Vanessa, says of her schedule, "When I stick to my workout on my schedule all week long, I feel so good about myself. I feel like a million bucks. Even if I don't immediately lose twenty pounds, I feel better and have more confidence. The feeling after a workout helps me to remember to stick to it the next week, thanks to the positive attitude it gives me."

• **Use the buddy system.** Find a friend, or an Ethel, to work out with on a regular basis. Work out a schedule that is agreed on by both of you and make a commitment to stick to it. Knowing you have a buddy there when you rise at five in the morning will help motivate you. On some days, it may be your buddy pushing both of you harder in your workout; on others, it may be you who's doing the urging. Either way, a buddy in it with you is a terrific motivator.

We have found we stick to our schedule more consistently and are able to stick to our workouts when we have each other. We also like to record each other's attendance to our buddy exercise dates. Not only are we more accountable for our behavior, but we also have to answer to someone else.

If you have an exercise buddy:

Make an exercise log using a calendar to record when your buddy sticks to her dates. Buy two calendars so you can each make your separate recordings.

Get together at the beginning of each week and decide when your exercise dates will be for the whole week. Just like we said above, stick to them!

Check in with each other after a month and see who has been the most diligent.

Think of a reward for the buddy who sticks to the schedule; perhaps whoever loses has to take the other out for dinner!

• **Avoid the quick fix.** Now that we're getting you pumped up about your exercise routine and your healthier lifestyle, we'd like to caution you about what not to do. Avoid the quick fix. Restrictive diets and budgets don't work. We'll get to budgets later in this book, but for now, we'll tell you why we believe diets are a bad idea. Some may work for a short time, but the lasting results don't hold a candle (or a slinky, tight-fitting dress!) to the results you find after you've committed to a healthier lifestyle and good eating habits. If you've been on more than one diet and aren't the size you think you should be, there's the proof that diets don't work. It's time to realize the only thing that does work is proper nutrition and consistent exercise.

Learning how to eat and exercise is a way of life, as we said above. Trendy diets are all extreme ways to fix a physical condition that can be permanently fixed by adjusting your lifestyle and giving yourself more time to work out and less opportunity to eat poorly.

Avoid diets and concentrate on developing habits that you can stick with your whole life. Moderation is the key to happiness. Eating moderately, working out moderately, and avoiding extreme quick fixes will help you stay balanced and centered.

- **Find out what exercise suits you.** It's time to choose your exercise program. Be careful and thoughtful about this. A program or exercise routine should be the *right fit* in order to *get you fit*. Trying to force yourself into a workout routine that doesn't suit your physical abilities or isn't enjoyable for you is setting yourself up for disaster. You will be less likely to keep to your routine if you don't enjoy what you are doing.

  Take a moment to think. Was there a sport or something in particular in gym that you enjoyed when you were younger? Is there something you were good at? Maybe you were on the track team or enjoyed tennis. Examine your physical abilities. If you are not all that coordinated and enjoy being alone when working out, an aerobics/dance class probably isn't for you: Something like swimming or running may be what you enjoy. Find a physical activity you are passionate about. Maybe you don't like to sweat and do vigorous sports and are more in tune with yoga. Regardless of what your interests and abilities are, there is something that is suited for you. Exploring different types of workouts may lead you to new hobbies and friends, a trimmer waistline, and a better self-image.

Stay at Homework: Grab your GAL Diary and write down five activities that you are interested in. Here are some to get you started:

Running

Walking

Biking

Aerobics

Spinning

Yoga

Pilates

StairMaster

Swimming

Tennis

Mountain biking

Basketball

Softball

CHOOSING YOUR EXERCISE ENVIRONMENT

Identify your exercise temperament and build a weekly routine around it. Your temperament may fall under one of the following:

1 You prefer an outdoor-based exercise routine. You'd rather walk, run, or bike outside than go to the gym. Stationary bikes and videotapes can be very effective if it rains and you want to exercise anyway.

2 You prefer a gym-based routine. You like going to the gym and having access to the social life, steam room, sauna, and machines.

3 You like a combination of gym activities and outside workouts.

Whichever preferences you have, this week you will begin your regimen.

Are You a Gym Gal?

If you choose to try a gym, be aware of the types of facilities. Here are some tips:

1 Are you more comfortable working out with women only? There are plenty of gyms with women-only memberships. Curves International is a great example.

2 If you prefer being in a coed gym, inquire as to this aspect before you join.

3 Make sure the gym you choose is convenient to your home. If you have to drive forty-five minutes out of the way, it will be easier to make excuses not to exercise. Is the gym convenient to other places you typically go (i.e., grocery store, kids' school)?

4 Make sure the gym offers the features, equipment, and atmosphere you're interested in. Be sure to take a tour and try out the facility before you join. Do classes cost extra? Do instructors have physiology degrees or other certification? Is the gym clean and well-maintained?

5 If you think you may have your kids with you during your workouts, look for a gym that has a day care center and qualified staff to babysit while you work out.

Are You an Outdoor Gal?

If you prefer the outdoors, there are many workouts to choose from: running, power walking, and biking, among others. You will be invigorated when you spend time being active outside. For many outdoor exercises, there are clubs that bring together people who enjoy the same activity. Seeking out these clubs is a good way to find a buddy. Local papers across the country advertise activities such as hiking, cycling, running, sailing, and tennis for clubs seeking members. Find a club that interests you and check it out.

If you choose to do an outdoor program, you should

- supplement your routine with videos to use when bad weather strikes. We have some suggestions of great videos on our Web site.

- get some free weights to use at home (start with 5- to 10-pound weights).

- commit to at least three days a week, as we said above.

Outdoor programs work, even when you have your child with you. One of our moms, Tammy, says, "I am a runner. I have always been a runner. When necessary, my daughter runs with me in a jogging stroller. She loves the outing and I love the results. My image in the mirror is my motivation. When I start to look soft or feel winded in a routine task, I am more motivated to hit the road more often."

Find the Right Program

Finding a program that suits you is important, if you feel you need more than just regular workouts. On our Web site, we have listed a host of successful programs we trust. Check them out and figure out which one is right for you. Below are a few programs we have had experience with and that MomsTown members have seen results from:

Gym Program Options

Curves: With more than seven thousand locations, it only takes thirty minutes! Curves not only guides you through a thirty-minute workout, but also has nutritional advice available: www.CurvesInternational.com.

Jazzercise: The focus here is on cardio, strength, stretching, and flexibility. And the classes incorporate music and dance to keep workouts lively and interesting. Get your groove. There are six thousand franchises teaching Jazzercise classes across the United States: www.Jazzercise.com.

Spinning: These popular classes are found in health clubs across the country. Not only do licensed instructors offer classes that constantly increase challenge and variety, but they also have developed an eight-week weight-loss program: www.Spinning.com.

Book Program Options

The World's Fittest You: Four Weeks to Total Fitness, **by Joe Decker, Eric Neuhaus:** This book is a perfect companion for the outdoor lover. You can have a great cardio/strength-training balance and do it all without a gym. Set up on a weekly basis, it includes recipes and tips.

Pain Free for Women: The Revolutionary Program for Ending Chronic Pain, **by Pete Egoscue:** The Egoscue Method is for women to use as safe, effective, and permanent relief from chronic pain without prescription painkillers, physical therapy, or invasive surgery. He shares his specially adapted "Pain Free" program for women to use at home. This is a great book, even if you don't have any physical pain.

Winsor Pilates and yoga tapes: Both are great alternatives to hitting the road or the gym. They wake up your body at the beginning of the day and de-stress and relax the body for sleep.

Personal Trainer Options

If you really want to jump-start your workout, a personal trainer is a great way to make sure you keep your appointments—because you're paying for them. If you don't have funds to do it on a regular basis, try it for just one or two sessions to get you going in the right direction. Also, employ the buddy system. Many trainers will give discounts on their fee when two or more want to train together.

Regardless of What You Choose, Commit to It This Week

Our friend Debbie found she enjoyed running outside and began to do it regularly, three to four times a week. She began to get bored doing the same run every day by herself and decided she needed a buddy. She explored her local running club and found another stay-at-home mom who ran regularly and lived in a neighborhood close by. The two explored other routes and eventually ran a 10K together. They developed a passion for running and worked toward achievements in their daily workouts. They eventually ran together in a marathon this past year.

Be creative about finding ways to work out that suit you. One of our moms, Lisa, started an exercise club just for SAHMs. It's called Stroller Strides, and all of the moms come with their kids and their strollers. Trained and certified as a physical trainer and nutritionist, Lisa takes all of the mothers through cardio and strength-training regimens using their strollers. It entertains their kids and gets them fit! She now has a franchise that has divisions throughout the country. Check out her Web site: www.strollerstrides.com.

◆ Tips for Beginning Your New Regimen ◆

• **Don't become a cardio-queen and forget strength training.** Comfort is a cage. When we feel comfortable with one kind of exercise, we often forget to do others. Remember to pursue a well-rounded regimen. If you're comfortable with running, walking, or aerobics but you don't lift weights, work free weights into your schedule. It can make all the difference. A recent study found that women who strength-train three times a week on average were able to increase their rate of metabolism by 15 percent. That averages out to two to three hundred more calories burned each day![*]

• **Interval training can be a great way to shock your body into change.** If you regularly walk, run, swim, or do a cardio machine at the gym,

---

[*]*Prevention: Healthy Woman,* 2004, p. 55

try inserting harder-paced, more strenuous intervals for three minutes at a time, five minutes apart into your workout. Do this several times during the session. You will find that your body responds better to physical variation than to repetitive, dull-paced exercise routines.

- **Mix it up.** Don't get stuck doing one thing every time you go to the gym. Try new workout classes and different outdoor activities. Be adventurous on the machines. You don't want to get bored with your "same ol' routine."

- **Little challenges are good for your daily routine.** Take the stairs, do crunches or push-ups in the morning, or fit in ten-minute walks here and there. Park a little farther away than you usually do to fit in a walk. Never underestimate the importance of each second of exercise you can fit into your schedule.

GET HEART SMART

Developing a healthy lifestyle means being aware of the crucial challenges your body faces as it gets older. Better heart health is one of the many benefits of our MomsTown workout philosophy. Many moms are unaware that heart disease and heart attacks are women's health problems. As moms, we worry so often about everyone else's health, we rarely think of how these things affect us. Keeping the heart healthy is important for both your physical and your emotional well-being. Doing aerobic exercise is crucial. One study found that women who walked for a total of one hour per week had a noticeably lower risk of heart attack. They also found stress reduction and better sleeping habits followed.

The heart has been called the "female organ" when it comes to emotions. Lisa Callahan, M.D., made the association that the heart is truly a female organ because, like women, it never takes a break. You know how that feels when pressure and stress don't allow rest and regular attention to your health. If you do not give yourself exercise, you are putting more pressure on your heart. Think about how that makes you feel as the mother, wife, and woman of the home.[*]

One of our moms, Katie, says, "Heart health is a big issue for me because my father, grandfather, and uncle all suffered heart attacks. I take working out seriously, and I encourage my husband and kids to be active all year round. We try to schedule family vacations that will allow us to hike, bike, and swim. My family's health is one of the main reasons I work out and have them do the same."

A Healthy Lifestyle Equals More Energy

A benefit from a consistent workout schedule is increased energy. When they make the time to work out, many of our MomsTown members experience more energy to face the other demands and pressures of a typical day. You owe it to yourself and your family to get fit. If you're lethargic, moody, and uninspired, the quickest fix is to get moving. Below are some tips on making healthier choices in nutrition that will increase your energy, your workout stamina, and your overall Body Attitude.

Interestingly enough, the principles that are effective for a successful exercise routine are the same principles for eating well: They are

---

[*]Lisa Callahan, M.D., *The Fitness Factor: Every Woman's Key to a Lifetime of Health and Well-Being*, Lyons Press, 2002.

consistency and frequency, using the buddy system, and avoiding the quick fix.

Consistency: Plan your meals in advance, and you'll be more likely to eat properly. Then if you have one night that throws you off, such as going out to pizza with your son's soccer team or going to dinner on date night with your husband, make sure that three days leading up to that night are planned, healthy meals. Consistently eating properly can keep you ready for those nights when you splurge. Not splurging for any old reason allows you to splurge once in a while when you do have a reason. Consistent healthy eating and meal planning are ways to keep yourself on track. On Sunday, when you plan your workouts, plan your meals as well. If you have a plan to eat healthfully, you are a lot more likely to do it.

Frequency: Do you ever wonder how women who seem to eat all the time stay so thin or fit? That's their secret. Eating four to six small meals a day speeds up your metabolism and keeps it revving all day long. You'll have increased energy and decreased flab. Just make sure the little meals are healthy ones!

Buddy System: Find a girlfriend who is willing to commit to a lifestyle of healthy meal planning. Together you can encourage and inspire each other to stay on top of your commitment to eating four to six times a day and feeding your family better meals. As you plan your weekly workouts on Sunday, you can also help each other plan your meals for the week. Write them in on your schedule. If you can't find a buddy to plan meals with you, come to www.MomsTown.com and click on. We have a weekly dinnertime menu plan, complete with recipes and a grocery list.

You Show What You Eat

If you make a regular meal out of bread, potatoes, and sugary treats you might as well duct-tape them to your behind, because they will follow you wherever you go. At MomsTown we like to remind women that what you put in your mouth is 80 to 85 percent of the fitness equation. This can be a shocking revelation for many women, and usually is for our MomsTown ladies. That doesn't mean go on a diet. It's just a matter of paying attention to what you eat. Following are some tips for watching what you eat more closely.

Eating better foods is a sure way to boost your energy. Surrounding yourself with more vegetables, fruits, and whole grains is one way to make a positive change to your daily energy levels.

Refined sugar, white flour, and a lack of vegetables won't keep you going for very long. In fact, eating junk food will actually decrease your energy. One great way to judge your pantry is to see how many processed and packaged foods you eat. Having a Pop-Tart in the morning instead of oatmeal and fruit is one way to kiss your valuable energy good-bye. Eating an apple instead of a cookie or candy bar for a snack will increase your energy level. A healthy diet boils down to using common sense.

◆Here are a few GAL tips for building a healthier
lifestyle for yourself. ◆

• **If it's not there, you can't eat it.** Following the simple healthy lifestyle tips of more vegetables, fruits, and whole grains is as easy as throwing those junk foods out of your pantry and kitchen. Out of sight, out of mind, as they say. When you're making lunch for your kids, you may forget to make it for yourself. By three o'clock you could eat a horse— or half a bag of potato chips, for that matter! Make sure you don't have anything on hand that will tempt you. Have a bowl of fruit at the ready. If you surround yourself with healthier snack options, you'll eat healthier snacks. And guess what? So will your kids. One of our moms, Diane, says, "Now that I make apples available for snacks instead of Chee•tos, my kids and I have developed a taste for them. I actually find myself craving an apple! It's a good feeling not to want the junk food."

• **When you shop, stick to the perimeter of the grocery store.** Have you ever noticed that the best foods for you are around the edges of the grocery store? For the most part, the fresh produce, fish, chicken, meat, and dairy surround the inner aisles. These inner aisles are where you'll find processed, sugary snacks, junk cereal, canned high-salt foods, soda, frozen foods, ice cream, and candy. Why tempt yourself when you're in a hurry? Avoiding the central aisles will save you calories and time!

• **Don't take your kids grocery shopping if you can avoid it.** They'll just con you into buying junk.

• **Don't grocery-shop when you're hungry.** You'll end up impulse buying, and chances are it won't be healthy—and may even be chips or munchies, sugary snacks you can open when you get in the car. Have a piece of fruit before you go to the grocery store if you don't have time to eat a meal. If you can't get anything to eat and find yourself there, go to the produce section first and pick a piece of fruit you can eat after you check out.

• **Avoid big meals.** Little meals are more fun, because they are more frequent and they fit into your busy schedule. Don't fill up on a huge meal at breakfast, lunch, or dinner; it zaps your energy as all of your blood goes to your stomach to digest the food, rather than to your head where you need it. It's also nice to allow yourself to eat more often in smaller quantities.

• **Avoid artificial energy boosters.** Caffeine can be terrible for your energy level. It feeds on itself—the more you drink, the more you want. If you drink coffee or iced tea all day long, you are constantly being pumped up by an outside substance, and then deserted once the substance is out of your system. This stress-induced condition occurs when the adrenals—glands vital to maintaining energy, metabolism, and a strong immune system—are overworked.

• **Get in the habit of reading the nutrition facts at the grocery store**—before you bring the food into your house.

• **Fourteen super foods:** One of the checklists that we use to stock our pantry is the list of the 14 Super Foods created by Dr. Steven Pratt in *Super Foods RX: Fourteen Foods That Will Change Your Life* (HarperCollins, 2004). They are beans, blueberries, broccoli, oats, oranges, pumpkin, salmon, soy, spinach, tea (green or black), tomatoes, turkey (skinless breast), walnuts, and yogurt. To learn more about why these are super foods, check out the book.

• **Try to buy vegetables and fruits that have vibrant, natural colors,** like green (lettuce, spinach, broccoli, asparagus), red (tomatoes, peppers, red lettuce, beets, apples), and orange (peppers, citrus fruits). The more bright colors there are on your plate, the more fresh, nonpackaged foods you will have.

As moms we've all experienced exhaustion, mood swings, and joyous chocolate cravings; however, they are taxing to our bodies. To boost your energy, consider the following:

Find natural energy boosters. If you need an energy boost, reach for natural herb teas and green tea instead of coffee and other caffeinated drinks. Green tea has terrific antioxidants and boosts energy levels without leaving you feeling drained. The late afternoon is a good time to have some to get you through dinner and the evening.

Eat breakfast. Make sure your meal includes protein, fat, and complex carbohydrates. Try a few egg whites, a slice of avocado, and a slice of whole grain toast. This meal will fire up your metabolism and get you ready for the day. If you don't have time to coordinate all of that and need a quick fix, choose oatmeal or fruit.

Taking vitamins is a good way to boost your immune system and energy. Next time you have a checkup, ask which vitamins your doctor recommends. Calcium is a must, and vitamins C, E, and B-12 are great. See if your doctor recommends a good, trusted multivitamin. Ask before taking vitamin E. Studies show that the oft-taken dose of 400 milligrams increases risk for hemorrhagic stroke.

H_2O is the way to go. Drink your water! Live by it, allow it to cleanse your body and rehydrate you. We often eat when we are actually just thirsty. Next time you want to eat when it isn't time for a snack or meal, drink a glass of water first and see if you feel as hungry. Start your day with a glass of water. Being tired all the time or not having enough energy can be signs of chronic dehydration. How much you drink depends on how active you are. If you're beginning a new workout, consider yourself active. For the amount you should drink, multiply .04 by your weight and then double it; that's how many glasses you should drink per day. Here is an example. Say you weigh 150 pounds: $150 \times .04 = 6$ and $6 \times 2 = 12$ glasses of water. One basic way to monitor if you are drinking enough water is to watch the color of your urine. When it is clear or light yellow and there is a lot of it, you've had enough to drink; if it's scant and dark yellow, you are most likely dehydrated. If it's too much to figure out the pounds-to-ounces equation, then just go grab a gallon of water and you're well on your way (to better health, and the bathroom several times a day).

Developing energy-boosting habits will help you fit more into your schedule, and will leave you feeling more enthused and passionate about what is possible. You deserve more energy, your new routine and your new life will call for it, and let's face it: When you have more energy, you feel great. You have leftover energy to do things for yourself, to make your workout, to put in time in your home office rather than just collapse in a heap on the couch every free minute you get. Boosting your energy through a series of lifestyle changes will ultimately change your overall attitude for the better.

Looking the Part Matters

Working out deserves respect, not only on your calendar and in your schedule, but also in your closet. If you go out of your way to have clothes that you have specifically purchased to work out in, you'll be more inclined to exercise than if you wear one of your big, baggy, stained T-shirts and a pair of sweatpants. There are a few reasons to get new workout clothes if you don't have them already. Remember, this doesn't have to clean out your bank account. Getting exercise clothes can mean going to Target or Wal-Mart, where affordable, attractive athletic wear is always available.

Practical reason for going shopping: Yes, we are concerned about our looks, but there is a practical element to this as well. Today's workout clothes are designed for breathability and movement. You are accommodating your activity by getting the proper clothes.

Feeling good about yourself: As for your new, workout-girl appearance, you will look and feel the part. As you start shaping up, you will enjoy seeing the changes occur in your body. It will be a lot more fun in a cute workout top that accentuates your figure.

Feeling like you belong: You will also feel you belong with your fellow workout peers in your gym or the running club. Often when we are beginning something, we feel like an impostor or an outsider. Preparing yourself from head to toe will help give you the confidence you need to feel like a legitimate, fit member of the active lifestyle club. That and a lot of sweat, hard work, and dedication will have you looking like a fit Gal in no time!

Record Your Successes

Make a point of recording, after each session, when you work out and what you do. Being able to look back and see the beginnings of a workout schedule blossom into progress feels good. You can use the exercise log/calendar that you share with your buddy. If you don't have a buddy, keep one for yourself.

Watch your energy soar and be aware of how it affects your posture, moods, and how others see you. You are on your way to becoming the Gal you've always wanted to be, and looking the part is half the battle.

Being committed to getting in shape for a healthier life shows your children, your friends, and your husband that you are worth it! We at MomsTown are passionate about how we look and feel, and that makes a difference in our quality of life. If you are not making a regular effort to work out and get fit, you are not giving your body the attention it deserves. If you want a long, healthy life with your family and friends, making the necessary changes and commitment is the only way to get it.

WEEK 4 SUMMARY

1. Remember that you are not just beginning a workout regimen, you are beginning a new kind of lifestyle—the MomsTown lifestyle! You will have more energy, confidence, and purpose, and your overall health will benefit in countless ways.

2. Pinpoint what part of the BABS syndrome you have. What areas do you want to improve (boobs, abs, butt, or all three)?

3. Recognize what excuses you use regularly to avoid sticking to a workout. What are your "big buts"?

4. Assess what your Body Attitude is (Unchallenged, Drifter, or Vigorous) and remember the exercise GAL Mantras that fit your Body Attitude as you proceed this week.

5. Remember three of the most important GAL Exercise Rules:
   • Do a workout three days a week for at least 30 minutes a day.
   • Every Sunday, schedule these workouts in your organizer.
   • Your workouts are your lifeline and cannot be negotiated or changed.

6. Remember to stick to consistent, frequent workouts. Begin this week with no excuses.

7. Establish a schedule and exercise log/calendar with a buddy.

8. Avoid quick fixes.

9. Find the type of exercise that best suits you. Make a list of exercises or physical activities you've always wanted to try.

10. Choose your exercise environment.

11. You show what you eat.
    - If it's not there, you can't eat it.
    - When you shop, stick to the perimeter of the grocery store.
    - Don't take your kids grocery shopping.
    - Don't grocery-shop when you're hungry.
    - Avoid big meals.
    - Avoid artificial energy boosters.
    - Get in the habit of reading the nutrition facts at the grocery store.

WEEK 5: MOMMY EINSTEIN—FROM MUSH TO MATTER

"**Problems cannot be solved** at the same level of awareness that created them," said Albert Einstein.

The MomsTown program, if done properly, will bring you to a new level of awareness. That awareness includes not only noticing and implementing new organizational routines, committing to a healthier lifestyle, and developing a workout regimen, but also assessing your mental outlook, beliefs, interests, and passions. This week we will concentrate on establishing an awareness of what your beliefs and interests are.

Natural Awareness Becomes Maternal Awareness

We know you already have an edge on awareness by virtue of being a mom. The MomsTown philosophy puts forth that you, as a mother, are capable of an enlightened awareness, or what we call maternal awareness. As moms, we know that once we birth a child we become a different woman. We all know it is not just that we are labeled "Mom." The inner transformation that takes place during pregnancy and when you first hold your baby brings with it a new and heightened awareness. It's the awareness that no babysitter or nanny can rival, because in the end, we know that no one will love our children quite as much as we do. This awareness can be expressed in the following ways:

- It is possible to distinguish our baby's cry from the cry of any other child in a crowded room full of children.

- We can sense when our babies are awake, even before the first fuss.

- Our protective instincts are heightened.

As we grow in our motherhood and we establish our habits, our boundaries and maternal awareness grow. Depending on what type of life we choose to lead, it can manifest in two different ways: contracted awareness or expanded awareness.

Contracted Awareness

Contracted awareness is a twisted, limited form of maternal awareness. Contracted awareness makes us feel a little crazy. It's the kind of attitude that some mothers exhibit—maybe friends you know, or even you—when they act out of fear and overprotection rather than level-headed parenting. The difference lies between taking responsibility for your kids' safety and limiting your family life with unnecessary fear. If you're operating your life from a constant contracted awareness, that's a problem. We are the primary role models for our children. Our fears not only limit them, but also shape them and their views of the world. When maternal awareness becomes contracted, our instincts are heightened and we become hyperaware of our environment. Many things around us begin to strike us as dangerous or threatening—a series of forces out to harm our children—even if they are not.

If you do not become aware of your overprotectiveness, you can potentially lose the respect of your family, kids, and friends. As one of our moms, Kim, observed, "I know women who insist on doing everything for their children. One of my friends practically chews her son's food for him. The sad thing is, he doesn't respect her for it. This attitude of disrespect rubs off on the rest of the household." Some moms perceive their environments and communities to be so extremely perilous that they stop taking risks, exploring options, and making smart choices. They become imbalanced as they listen to fear more than reason.

One of our moms, Maria, had three beautiful children, ages three, six, and nine, and an adoring husband. She became one of the most devoted moms in her group of friends—so devoted, in fact, that she never ventured out without her children, even for an occasional date with her husband. She feared that her children would not be okay without her. She could not trust a babysitter. She feared that she would not be a good mother if she left her children to go out and take time for herself. She used many excuses for avoiding social events. Three years passed, and her youngest began school and suffered temper tantrums and hysterical crying because he could not stand to be separated from his mother. Maria's husband began taking nights out with his friends without her and they grew apart. Their sex life suffered and so did their marriage. Maria had allowed her fear and contracted awareness to limit her life, herself, and her family.

A mom with contracted awareness is alarmed on many levels. She's afraid of germs, heights, bullies, terrorists, and letting go. Alarm and paranoia can become controlling factors that wreak havoc on us, our kids, and our husbands. Extreme contracted awareness can lead to insecure or rebellious children and a husband who wants to stray or withdraw. Let's face it: A woman who is afraid of everything isn't all that much fun to be around.

Another MomsTown mom, Tricia, observed detrimental effects of overprotectiveness in her family. "My nephew is nine years old and doesn't have a bike because my sister-in-law doesn't want him to learn how to ride one. She said she's afraid he will fall off while he's learning to ride and hurt himself, then once he learns to ride it she'll worry about his whereabouts all the time. She has a really hard time letting him out of her sight, even when they're at home. If he's in the yard playing, she'll sit on the porch and watch over him. She hardly ever allows him to go over to a friend's house to play unaccompanied. She even has a hard time letting him go places with his own grandparents . . . Basically this has made my nephew a wimp around other kids. He's very easily hurt or made to cry. He's also disrespectful of his mom because she watches his every single move. When she asks him what he's up to, he'll say, 'Nothing,' but the look on his face is saying, 'What the heck do you have to ask me every five minutes for?' and he'll roll his eyes before going back to play . . . Within the past year or so, though, he has become my brother's shadow . . . because when he's with my brother he's allowed to be a kid."

In varied degrees, we have all experienced less extreme versions of contracted awareness. Do any of these examples sound familiar to you, or do they fit any moms you know?

- The contracted mom lives in a routine. She lives on *Groundhog Day*. Every day is the same and she not only is afraid to break out of the routine but also finds security in the isolation.

- She comes to believe this is the only way to parent and the only way to be a good mom.

• She makes excuses for not attending parties.

• She avoids the girls' night out.

• She won't leave her kids with a babysitter.

• She won't allow her child to play any sport she perceives as dangerous.

• She allows fear to make her decisions for her and take over her judgment and instincts.

• Overprotective "motherly" instincts and actions begin to define who she is to her children, husband, and friends. This extreme behavior takes over her personal identity.

• She's a worrywart.

Our maternal awareness serves its purpose to protect our children, but not at the expense of our own well-being. When you stop exploring life due to your fears, you have stopped living your life for yourself. Not taking risks causes possibilities to be limited and your potential to be stymied. You not only affect yourself this way, you affect your kids in a negative, limiting way as well. In carrying out this program, we've seen contracted awareness in small and large ways with many moms. We tell these mothers, just as we told Maria, you must turn your contracted awareness into expanded awareness. Take a deep breath and face the world, and show your children how to do the same.

Expanded Awareness

At MomsTown, we aim for expanded awareness. Expanded awareness invites life, love, and potential into your home. You welcome new experiences, change, and adventurous choices. You make time for yourself and your husband because your happiness depends on it. You take educated risks. You go out on date night because it helps your soul and identity breathe, and for goodness' sakes, whether you like it or not, your kids need a break from you!

Here are some examples of educated risks:

• You allow a babysitter to stay with your kids for your weekly date night. You educate yourself by interviewing the babysitter and checking her references. You have a good feeling about her.

• You go to a party without your children. You reassure yourself that this does not mean you are neglecting them.

• You allow your little boy to play baseball. You equip him with appropriate gear, tell yourself that it is natural for little boys to always get scrapes and bruises.

• You make yourself see the world around you and choices you make objectively, rather than seeing them through a lens of paranoia and fear.

• You explore expanded awareness in small everyday ways, like allowing your kids to experience little surprises during their day. One of our moms decided to allow her children to have dessert before dinner one night. Her kids were so surprised they didn't know what to do. Another one of our moms decided to let her child pick the family activity for the weekend. It turned out to be going to a water amusement park. The family had a wonderful time. Letting go of control sometimes allows us more in the end. Other ideas for changing your daily routine and allowing a little unpredictability to enter into your daily decisions are 1) allowing your kids to plan the dinner menu once a month, 2) declaring a surprise day and taking your kids, blindfolded, to a surprise outing, and 3) letting them explore while you keep a watchful eye, but allowing them to figure things out.

Expanded awareness is when you trust yourself, trust your instincts, and trust you're doing the best job that you can. Expanded awareness is a willingness to explore options. Allow yourself to entertain possibilities and trust your judgment and instinct once you've taken fear out of the picture.

Stay at Homework: This week, try something out of the ordinary, whether it be going out on date night or letting the kids do something completely outside of their routine. Change is refreshing. You need it for balance, and so does your family.

We shared our contracted/expanded awareness philosophy with Maria, and she began to go out regularly on date night. At first it was difficult due to her kids' previous routine, but after a couple of weeks, it became easier and easier. Now she can't wait for date night, and her kids are excited to see the babysitter. She has begun using expanded awareness in her life decisions and keeping her fear at bay.

Other moms, like Molly, have confessed, "It is not easy to sit back and watch my daughter move headfirst toward something unpleasant (like bumping her head on the coffee table), but I think that she will become a better person if I can let her bump up against things in life and then learn how to avoid those things on her own."

DOES YOUR BRAIN FEEL LIKE MUSH?

What does it mean when your brain turns to mush? It means you've been talking to two-year-olds or even twelve-year-olds too long. We're not saying your children aren't interesting or intellectually stimulating, because we all know kids can test our mental capacity. We will say that motherhood can't satisfy ALL of your intellectual needs. You are an adult, a woman who deserves to keep learning and growing. If you are feeling the inner itch, that is a sign that something inside wants to live, be expressed. Be aware. This is normal and all you have to do is work some basic habits into your routine to get your intellect on track.

Finding interests of your own and pursuing them will light something in you. It's a matter of recognizing that spark and fanning the fire. We contend that a SAHM's discontent is due to the fire smoldering, waiting for a gust of inspiration. Look outside the house, beyond the laundry, and past the errands. This chapter will provide tips and exercises to get your synapses firing and ignite your dormant potential.

Wallflower to Wildflower

If you have ever found yourself in a social setting being asked, "Oh, what do you do?" your reply might be, "I'm a stay-at-home mom." Before you know it, the person who asked you the question is looking to talk with someone else. You have a choice; you can become a wallflower and stand passively next to your husband, nodding when appropriate, or you can transform yourself into a wildflower, popping up in conversations, chiming in with a tidbit of current news or a philosophy you find intriguing.

As a wildflower, you will find your life and interactions more expansive. As a wildflower, you contain seeds of possibility. And before you know it, you have a field of opportunities. Think of when you look at a field of wildflowers. It has variety, it's colorful, it's not especially symmetrical or uniform, and yet in some amazing way it's harmonious. We want you to be a wildflower, which means we want you to have your own field of interests, passions, ideas, and potential to cultivate that are unique to you.

In this chapter we encourage you to define your beliefs, opinions, values, and philosophy of life. Indulging your intellect will give you permission to try new interests, meet new friends, have confidence around strangers, and allow yourself to live more vivaciously. A person who knows what she believes and who she is, is more confident, daring, adventurous, and just plain more fun to be around.

Think back to subjects that you were drawn to as a child, including those in school, or extracurricular activities. At this point in your life, you may feel estranged from those interests. Be ambitious about your interests. Make them something you are familiar with, not only emotionally but also intellectually.

Stay at Homework: Grab your diary and write down three basic interests that you would like to become reacquainted with. Here are a few examples to get you started: art, film, gardening, yoga, environmental issues, politics, interior decorating, fashion, community development, music, literature, history, crafts, sculpture, cooking, painting, jazz, photography, bird-watching, quilting, tennis.

This week we will begin working on one of the interests you write down. Pick the one you would like to focus on. This is your officially designated Passion (with a capital *P*!). With your Passion, do the following GAL-ercise. Remember, we will work with this passion throughout the chapter, but it doesn't mean this is your ultimate passion. This can be your passion for this month. We want to keep the steps deliberate and exact and identify things you can fit into your life in practical, doable ways.

More than anything else, we are learning how to pursue passions. It is more about your pursuit and development of the passion than the nature of the passion itself.

Stay at Homework: Go online and find a specialty magazine that suits your passion, and order it—this week.

By taking small steps to uncover your interests and surround yourself with things that support your interests, you will begin uncovering your sense of passion, and your lust for learning will come back full force once you find your real dreams and interests and chase them with information. You will be empowered by all you take in. It will make you more excited to wake up in the morning.

Once you have identified which passion you'd like to focus on and indulge in, you can allow yourself the freedom to explore it in several ways. So often we keep ourselves from doing things to further our unique talents and passions. Be creative in the ways you explore your passion. Talking to those who share the same passion and ordering your magazine are a couple. Doing research on the Internet is another.

Stay at Homework: Google your interest on the Internet for fifteen minutes or more. Allow yourself to sit, undisturbed, and sift through the search-engine results on your passion. For those of you who might not Google very often, just use your passion as the keyword in the search.

One of our MomsTown members, Marcy, said of her new passion, "I always put off learning more about gardening and telling myself I didn't have enough time to devote to it because I have an active four- and seven-year-old. Once I made myself begin spending time on the Internet researching it, even for fifteen minutes, it reinvigorated my enthusiasm, and I actually found a gardening store listed on the Internet that wasn't far from my house. The next day, on the way back from the grocery store, I stopped into the store and got a new gardening tool and went straight home, brought the kids out in the yard to help me, and began digging a plot for some perennials. It felt wonderful and the kids had a great time. They bragged to their dad when he came home that they had helped begin our new garden."

We hear stories like this all the time about seemingly small developments that get women on track, doing things they enjoy. As small as some of these efforts may seem, they are essential to improving your quality of life and your daily experiences.

Bring Your Passion to Your Community

When you figure out what your passion is, you can bring it to your community, and chances are, your community can help you with it. Below are some ways you can support your passion. Some passions may fit some options better than others. Pick one of these activities and set it in motion this week.

- Find a class at a local community center, college, or university that suits your interest. Make that work for your schedule and work it out with your husband or a babysitter, or another mom (maybe your buddy), so that you are able to attend.

- Do some research to find out if there is a club or organization that supports your interest and join. If you can't find this in your community, do it online!

- See if any programs at your community center mesh with your passion. If not, perhaps you can propose starting a program.

• Check online for chat rooms, newsletters, and forums to join so you can connect with others who enjoy your passion. Online communities can be as interactive as local communities. The MomsTown message board is an active online community. It's easy to join. We invite you to pay us a visit at www .MomsTown.com/forum.

Another way to work toward being loyal to your beliefs and pursuing those interests is to allow your intellectual interests to breed action in social and community arenas. For example, if you are genuinely enthused about modern art, you have signed up for a subscription in the modern art magazine, and you have begun taking a class in art history or sculpture; now take it to another level. Is there a community art project that is in the works, is on the back burner, or needs to be initiated? Perhaps there are other people in the community who have the same interest and would like to be part of an annual or monthly art association. Taking the class on your subject of interest gives you a degree of knowledge and your passion gives you the direction and ambition to lead the association.

Our friend Susan is a stay-at-home mom with two kids. She had a passionate interest in finance and accountancy and a basic talent for numbers and math. After rediscovering her interests, she decided to take a course in business and accountancy, which led her to meet a professor who was very involved in a local business and looking for someone to do some part-time work on a new venture. She was able to work out of her home doing exactly what she loved. Her pursuit of her interests led her toward a business opportunity. She says of her passion, "Just taking a couple of beginner steps toward learning more led me to all sorts of opportunities and different people who shared my interest."

When you are proactive about your passion, not only will you feed your need to learn, stimulate your intellect, and grow creatively, but you'll have plenty to contribute to dinner conversation. You'll bring your own knowledge to the table! You will be amazed by how exciting it is to become involved, active, and knowledgeable about a subject that interests you.

Think About What You're Thinking: The Defining Topics

It is time to dust off your thoughts, opinions, values, and morals. Strength in morality, values, and personal beliefs adds to your confidence, attitude, and how you function as a role model for your children. If you're a SAHM or considering the MomsTown way of life by doing our program, you are setting yourself up for more than just taking care of the kids, pursuing work out of your home, and running the household. You are defining and becoming the person you want to be for yourself and as a role model for your children.

First things first. Let's figure out what your opinions and beliefs are. So often we assume that opinions and beliefs will be there when we need them. The truth is that they deserve attention and focus in order to flourish and become influential parts of your value system, your family, and your life.

Stay at Homework: Grab your diary and review the following topics. Write at least four sentences about each. Following each topic are some questions to get you started. Some topics may have a weekly GAL-ercise. Add that exercise to your schedule.

Religion/Spirituality

What do you and your family believe as far as values and religion?
Do you study and practice a particular religion? Or do you have
   a spiritual philosophy?
How does this fit in with your perception of who you want to
   become?

Have you actively questioned your spiritual beliefs in the past
six months?

By evaluating your personal feelings about religion and spirituality,
you are becoming aware of whether or not you need to focus on this in
your life to strengthen your beliefs.

GAL-ercise: In your organizer, schedule a time this week to sit for
fifteen minutes before bed or upon waking to consider what your religious or spiritual beliefs mean to you on a regular basis. If you find you
draw a blank, think about what you ideally want your beliefs to be and
how they can become a part of your daily life.

Politics

It is not unusual for children to adopt the political opinions of their
parents. Even if they don't, it is essential for you to know where you
stand enough to have an educated reason as to why you believe or vote
the way you do. In this section ask:

What are your political beliefs? Are you loyal to a political
party?
What do you think about the hot button issues in the news to-
day? Choose one and explain what your stance is.
Is there a particular issue you are passionate about? Name two.
Have you voted? If so, why did you choose a particular candi-
date?
Are you proud of what you believe? Why or why not?

Know what you believe and why you believe it so you can be a confident, active participant.

GAL-ercise: During the next local or national election, you must vote. If your children are old enough, take them to your polling place with you. Explain the importance of voting. Exercise your right to influence your world and shape history.

Love

Recommit to taking care of yourself first so you are able to extend that love to your family and friends. When we express how important a person is to us and how much we appreciate them, we strengthen the bond to that person. Besides, it feels good to share loving comments with another.

How do you express your love in everyday ways to your children? To your husband? To your extended family? To your friends?

How do you show you love yourself? Name three ways.

In what ways do you pamper yourself? Name three ways.

If you can't list the ways you take care of yourself, make up one that you would like to begin doing and do it today.

GAL-ercise: In your diary, write down three people you would like to express your love to this week. You can do this with a phone call, a card, or just a hug when you see them next time.

Family Values and Morals

It is time now to focus on values and morals. Values and morals are important to keep the family moving in a unified direction. Values can be action oriented and tell the world what you deem worthy of your attention, energy, and regard. Values help you keep your priorities in line. Examples of things you value could be time, money, environment, or marriage. List three things you value and tell why they are important to you and your family.

Morals are the character, teaching, and exhibiting of goodness and responsible behavior. They arise from your sense of right and wrong.

> Can you define what you stand for and what establishes meaning in your life?
>
> What are the priorities in your family? (family, time with each other, money)
>
> Is it a priority to spend quality time or quantities of time?
>
> List three examples of your family morals.
>
> Are you hypocritical in an area of your life? Everyone is! Try to name at least one example.
>
> Do you gossip, have discriminatory thoughts, or make such comments about others?
>
> Do you judge others unfairly? If so, how do you find yourself doing it most often?

These are hard questions to ask yourself and it's possibly even harder to be honest with the answers. But only when we recognize our own faults do we see room for improvement.

GAL-ercise: This week, next time you notice yourself judging someone, mentally or verbally, hold back. Consider why you are judging.

Attitude/Outlook

Are you an optimist or a pessimist? Chances are you have a pretty good idea what you are. If you are unsure, ask:

Do you assume you will be successful, or do you expect some modicum of failure?

Do you meet challenges head-on, or do you avoid them as long as possible?

Do you wake up enthusiastic and excited about the day?

Do you feel your best days are behind you or yet to come?

Weekly Exercise: In your diary name two things you will work on being positive and optimistic about.

Money

Since there is a whole chapter devoted to this topic we will ask just a few questions to ready you for the real work to be done later. For starters,

Do you want more money?

On a scale of 1 to 10, 1 being least important, where does money rank in priority to you?

What is the number-one reason you want money in your life?

Assess Your Answers

Read over the sentences you have written about each of the defining topics.

Do you sound as if you know where you stand with all of the
above?

Do you seem to be someone who is actively pursuing her interests and beliefs on a regular basis?

Stay at Homework: This week, choose one of the above topics and commit
to exploring your beliefs on that topic. You must schedule fifteen minutes
on the computer Googling your particular interests in the defining topic of
your choice. Put it on your calendar and follow through by doing it.

One of our MomsTown members, Jenny, said, "I really do feel that I
have beliefs and convictions for all of the defining topics, but I so rarely
allow myself to dwell on them that they get lost in the shuffle of daily
life. Just taking time out to focus on a few of the topics, I found myself
more aware on a regular basis as to whether or not I was a role model for
my children in all sorts of ways, from making religion and spirituality
a part of our family life by discussing it openly to making sure I vote.
It made a difference when I took time to evaluate the defining topics. I
became more self-aware of who I am and who I want to be."

Like Julie, so many moms get busy with just getting through their
daily schedules. To get it all, we believe one of the essential things that
makes this program effective for you is that you stick to the commitments
you make on your schedule, like time on the Internet, with your diary,
or thinking. These activities will put you in touch with yourself and your
passions. If you can follow through with your Stay at Homeworks, you
will begin to see the difference in your attitude!

The Fine Print

The best opinions are informed and educated ones. The simplest
way to back your opinions and develop new ones is to stay abreast of
current events. Decide to read a publication as part of your daily routine.

Stay at Homework: This week, read this publication for fifteen minutes each day. Put it on your calendar. If you don't feel you can fit it into your daily routine, wake up fifteen minutes early and do it directly after making your bed and picking your Hot Iron. Here are some choices for your news source:

* Get the local paper delivered.

* Get a national paper delivered.

* Sign up for an e-mail newsletter from the daily news publication of your choice (the *New York Times*, the *Wall Street Journal*, the *Washington Post*, *Salon*, the local paper, CNN.com).

Since time is of the essence, you can scan all of the headlines first and then go back and read the articles that interest you. Don't try to force-feed yourself a whole morning paper and then berate yourself when you can't finish it.

Reading the paper each morning will feed your mental cravings. Try to avoid looking at it as another chore. Being in touch with current events is an activity that keeps you in tune with the rest of the world. The more you know, the more your children will know. And you might actually enjoy it! Most of our moms find reading the paper fits into their schedule nicely after they have made their bed, chosen their Hot Iron, and prioritized their schedule. Skimming the headlines is a great exercise to do next, before your day heats up.

Candace says of her newfound newspaper reading practice, "At night when my husband gets home and we are having dinner, I love to bring up topics I read about in the local paper. I find that my husband may not have had time to hear about certain current events and is interested in hearing my opinion about them. Since I've begun reading the paper, he defers to me on current-event knowledge and it feels great. Even if I have been with the kids all day, I have new topics to bring up at dinner that may have local or national relevance. I have developed the habit of skimming the headlines even if I don't have time to read them— it makes me feel less like I'm missing out by being at home."

Reading a newspaper or online source of news every day is an easy way to develop opinions backed by knowledge.

Help Your Kids Read the Fine Print

If your children are old enough, you can help them develop knowledge and interest in current events. Here are a few ways to fit this into your day.

- Go over the headlines with them at the breakfast table in the mornings. We don't suggest you go over the details of the *Wall Street Journal*, but going over the headlines can be as simple as "NASA is sending a spaceship to Mars tomorrow!" Use your judgment to find current events that might pique their interest.

- Pick one topic and relate the event to your kids in easy-to-understand terminology some time during the day.

- Find cities and countries on the map or globe with your children when they become hot topics in the news. It will stimulate discussion and add to your and your children's education.

Making news and current events part of your family life can help your children shape their own opinions and will send them into the world informed and better prepared. It's also a way for you to continue learning and discovering on a daily basis.

SAHM Amnesia

Stay-at-home moms often complain that since having children, their minds have turned to mush and they often forget things. One of our moms, Krissy, told us, "I was appointed PTA vice president once. I set up an orientation meeting for the previous year's board and the incoming board. Everybody showed up for it—except me!"

Yes, moms do forget things. We'll admit, there is truth to this, but it doesn't have to stay that way. Your mind is agile and efficient, and if you want to be more alert and have more intellectual stimulation, the only thing standing in your way is your own perceived limitations. Last year, Heather and her husband actually forgot their anniversary! It shocked both of them. Between work, the kids' school commitments, friends, and family, it was lost in the shuffle. Often forgetting a big event like that is a wake-up call that you need to give your schedule and organizational methods (and possibly your relationship with your husband) more attention. It is also important not to be too hard on yourself when you inevitably forget.

One MomsTown member, Fran, said, "I forget things all of the time. Now I finally understand why I sometimes thought my own mother was a complete flake when I was little. With the kids and all of our schedules, there just isn't enough room in my brain for everything anymore. Part of it is the fact that there is suddenly so much to do just to get through the day. So even when I remember what I am supposed to do at that moment, on the way to do that, I run into three or four things that demand equal attention, and before I know it, I've forgotten what my original task was."

Forgetting is just part of being a mom. That's a fact, but it can be curtailed by strong organizational methods. When you do forget, you can't beat yourself up for it. It's hard to remember every engagement your kids have, your obligations, your husband's obligations, your friends' birthdays, and even your kids' friends' birthdays. Frankly, it is impossible. But there are things you can do to avoid frequent forgetfulness. Organization is a key element of conquering forgetfulness. You can figure out a system for remembering your daughter's ballet recital, the school bake sale, your appointment with a new client, *and* everyone's birthday.

Some moms just have difficulty getting out of the door with everything they need. Said one mom, Lorie, "Once I'm out of the house, it's remembering everything that poses the problem. I can usually get all of my daughter's stuff together, but I sometimes find I am out and about and my list of stops is still sitting on the entrance-hall table."

Earlier in the book, we discussed getting an organizer as being crucial to your success and your commitments. Our program encourages and reminds you to be aware of treating your commitments and your life with professional respect in the most basic, simple ways. Grab your organizer and do the following:

- Write reminders of all of your family's and friends' birthdays on your calendar. Note the actual day, but also write a reminder in two weeks ahead of time.

- When you receive invitations to weddings, write the date on your calendar, but also write a reminder as to how early you need to book and schedule travel plans, accommodations, etc. If possible, this should be up to three months ahead of time.

- As soon as you make doctor appointments for your kids or you, write them down.

• Use brightly colored stickers to denote regular events, including:

Newborns' shots

Little League games

Ballet lessons

Dentist appointments

• When you know you're going out, begin getting everything ready early. Put things by the door as you think of them. You can even begin doing this the night before if you have to leave early in the morning and know you need quite a few things for your errands.

As you work toward cutting down on the forgetfulness and having a more organized schedule you honor and respect, try to remember that mistakes happen and everyone forgets; even though you're a goddess, remember, you're also human!

Learning Every Day

Below are some strategies and topics to consider in your world around you. If you make a point to be aware of these topics, you will find more power and clarity in your daily life. As you become more familiar with your interests and passions, and read more, here are some things to keep in mind.

How do you learn? One of the most important things to examine is what is best for you when you are learning. Are you better at learning visually, verbally, reading, or maybe even listening to audiotapes? Become aware of how you pick up things most easily.

What do you enjoy reading? Are you a fan of mysteries, romances, pop fiction, true crime, historical fiction, or nonfiction? Pinpoint what you are drawn to and know what you like.

Stay at Homework: Grab your GAL Diary and write down five of your favorite books. It's okay if you need to go all the way back to grade school to remember. *Charlotte's Web* counts!

As you recall these books, allow yourself to remember how good it felt to read a terrific book and get completely absorbed in the story. You deserve to be able to do that now! Even if you're exhausted, everyone can allow herself at least a few minutes before bed to read. Or even better, find a good book your children will enjoy, too, and read a chapter aloud before their bedtime. The most wonderful thing about books is that they awaken the imagination. In this program, we will be doing several things to get that imagination going. When your imagination is alive, you are more creative, energetic, fun to be around, and make a much better play pal for your kids!

Stay at Homework: Go to your local library. If you don't have a library card, sign up for one this week. Check out at least two items. Depending on what appeals to you, choose a book or an audiotape of a good book. Figure out what you enjoy reading and try some new genres. If you've always read mysteries, try a romance. If you have always been drawn to fiction, try a nonfiction book. Allow yourself to be adventurous and see what happens! You may discover a whole new passion.

Know your favorite newspapers and magazines. Which one appeals to your sensibilities, politics, and lifestyle? Having a favorite rather than trying to get to all of them defines your outlook more and makes you saner. Having a favorite newspaper and magazine also drives you to read and seek out information more often. Earlier in the chapter, we suggested finding a newspaper that appeals to your sensibilities and looking over it every day.

Stay at Homework: If you cannot think of three magazines or periodicals you enjoy reading, take some time this week to go to Barnes & Noble or

Borders and leaf through the periodicals and magazines. Try to find three you enjoy. We don't want you to subscribe to all three. If you like, subscribe to one. Flooding your mailbox with magazines is not the objective here. This is an exercise to get you out to a bookstore, actively seeking out reading material that appeals to you. Take the kids and let them visit the kids' section—most of these bookstores have departments with toys and a terrific selection of kids' books. Exposing your kids to books rather than arcade games sets the right example.

Become familiar with technology. Are you comfortable using the Internet? Are you comfortable Googling or doing a search whenever you need something? If you are at home most of the time, technology is an invaluable tool connecting you to the outside world. Instead of watching that soap opera or talk show, take the time to do a Google search. Make yourself an expert on the Internet. It will become one of your most powerful allies.

Stay at Homework: If you have a favorite show that comes on during the day, skip it the next time and spend that time on the computer surfing the Net. It's a lot more interesting, we promise. Wouldn't you rather consider yourself computer savvy than an expert on *Days of Our Lives*?

Stay at Homework: If you do not have an e-mail account, register for one this week. It doesn't have to cost anything. You can sign up for Hotmail or Yahoo accounts for free. This way, you can correspond with your friends and family, and receive news, specialty newsletters, and more.

Improve your vocabulary. Learn a new word every day or every week. Share it with your children and help them use it in the proper context.

Stay at Homework: Sign up for a daily or weekly vocabulary word from Merriam-Webster online at www.m-w.com. Don't worry, it's free! Do it today.

As you make subtle changes to your outlook, evaluate your beliefs, and become more proactive in exploring areas of interest and the world around you, you take small but important steps toward getting the life you want and feeling more confident about yourself. Discovery and knowledge will do wonders for your self-confidence and your passion about your life, family, and children. By sticking with our program, you will see differences in your outlook and your interactions with people. You will be a step closer to getting it all!

WEEK 5 SUMMARY

1. Make your bed every day!

2. Follow through on your workouts three times a week.

3. Pick an item from your Anti-Clutter list and tackle it this week.

4. Try a break from your routine this week. Make it an adventure in expanded awareness with an educated risk.

5. Choose your passion for this month and begin to do things to learn about it. Do research on the Internet about your passion. Check out a community club or Internet forum that addresses it.

6. Order a paper (on the Internet or a hard copy) and begin reading it every morning.

7. Start scheduling things you'll need to remember in your organizer (birthdays, anniversaries, weddings, appointments, etc.).

8. Sign up for a vocabulary word of the week/month to be delivered to your e-mail account.

WEEK 6: GETTING IN TOUCH WITH YOUR SPIRITUALITY

GETTING ENGAGED

We believe the MomsTown blueprint will lead you to a lifestyle, a philosophy, an inner strength, and an attitude. Getting it all is more than getting organized, exercising, and developing your interests; it's about the transformation of your very being. This week we'd like to focus on balancing your spirituality, finding your virtues, authenticity, humility, courage, hope, and inspiration. Once you begin exploring these elements of yourself, you will gain a dynamic sense of power and strength. Spirituality in the MomsTown context is being true to the person you are inside and finding who that person is. Religion may be a part of your beliefs. We strongly believe that spirituality is about engaging your heart in the way you think and in the way you act.

The GAL Sanctuary

The GAL Sanctuary is a place we are going to ask you to create inside yourself, and physically in your home. The GAL Sanctuary is a retreat where you will go once a day to refresh, rejuvenate, refuel, reenergize, replenish, refine, remember, recover, and reengage. The GAL Sanctuary is your haven.

We suggest making a special place in your home where you can be alone for at least fifteen minutes a day. Just as with your home office, this is a specific, designated place where you do particular work. With your office it is bills, organizational tasks, and paperwork. In the GAL Sanctuary you work on you. The sanctuary is not a place where you focus on the kids, your husband, your stress, or anything you think you need to be doing, but simply you.

Your GAL Sanctuary is your secluded space. It is not necessarily a religious space—unless that is what you want. This space represents what makes you stronger, what makes you feel reconnected. Every sanctuary will be unique. *Sanctuary* stands for what feels good to you and speaks to your sense of self. One of our moms, Katie, said of spending time in her sanctuary, "I finally set aside some time and found that taking time out of my day to spend in my sanctuary cleared my mind, made me feel ready to take on anything, and gave me perspective. I actually felt refreshed. I started making a habit of doing it when my son was taking a nap."

First things first: You need to set up your GAL Sanctuary so that it fits your personality. Creating a sanctuary does not mean spending a lot of money, building an addition onto your home, or altering the layout of the house. It means finding a place where you can be alone for fifteen minutes of the day and clear your mind. Here are some things to keep in mind as you establish your sanctuary.

• Pick a place that is not usually occupied by children or guests during the day. Your bedroom is a good place, since it is usually the closest to your intimate space. It can be a corner or a three- to four-foot span of bare wall or carpet.

• This corner or part of your bedroom does not have to be permanently altered in any way. When you are finished with your sanctuary you can disassemble your sanctuary accessories.

• The makeup of a GAL Sanctuary can be simple. It can consist of a piece of material, a blanket, or a yoga mat that you like. Setting out the material in your spot, you can arrange your sanctuary accessories around you. You can also get a comfortable pillow.

• Collect sanctuary accessories. These can be aromatherapy candles, essential oils, or any artifacts or items that are special to you. Sanctuary accessories can be childhood memorabilia, flowers, a special picture, or a figurine. Keep in mind as you gather these items that they will be brought out when you are ready to do your fifteen minutes of sanctuary time.

• Designate a time during the day that works for you. Morning is a great time—before the kids are awake.

• Set up your sanctuary, light your candles, sprinkle some essential oils, and take some deep breaths.

• Take a look at your watch and check the time. Stay in this place for fifteen minutes.

• Be patient. This process may feel uncomfortable for the first couple of days. It's like going on vacation. The first two days, you're still caught up in the rat race of your home, thinking of phone calls, e-mails, unfinished business, and what you will face during the day. With patience and determination, eventually you can melt it away. As with a vacation, the third day is when you sink into the rhythm of your destination. This will happen in your sanctuary if you give it time.

• Make sure you are in a comfortable position, legs crossed and relaxed.

• Allow yourself to be quiet. All of your stresses, worries, and fears can be allowed to drain away as you clear your mind. In the beginning, it may be tough to clear your mind, in which case just observe the thoughts that come through and don't let yourself become attached to them.

• Say your GAL Mantra fifteen times.

Stay at Homework: This week make time to establish your sanctuary. You can be as simple or extravagant as you like. You must spend at least fifteen minutes three times a week in it.

The Inner You

As you engage in the week, our goal is to help you engage your creative strength. This week is designed to awaken you to your inner knowledge, instincts, and power. We will assist you in delving into your resources—much of what your spirit knows to be true and your daily personality might need to learn. The MomsTown program brings your inner Gal to the outer realm of your daily life and attitude. One of our most important reminders with every step of our program has to do with balance and moderation. Throughout this week, we will be doing exercises to find out if your spirituality is in tune with your desires. If it isn't, then let's tune in. Following is a discussion of some principles to help you evaluate some of your spiritual elements.

Elegance

If there is one thing you should associate with your Gal, it's elegance. When we think of elegance we typically associate it with materialistic style, expensive clothes, jewelry, or fashion. We at MomsTown believe elegance is so much more. Elegance can be inherent in the way you respond to life. It is an inner quality that filters out the negative, fearful reactions we might have to any sudden situation, worry, or circumstance. By consciously choosing to be elegant throughout your day you learn to take a breath the split second before you respond to a stressful situation, thus exuding a poised, calm, and reassuring demeanor. To achieve this elevated and elegant air you must establish an inner safe place. This place houses your faith, hope, and positive attitude.

For example, if you are expecting a particular positive outcome to a situation and the results are the opposite, you might take a deep breath and say, "Maybe it wasn't meant to be." This is an elevated and elegant response. A non-elegant response is to get angry or try to manipulate others or the situation to get what you want.

Elegance is about taking your self-control and allowing it to elevate your whole being. It's about having positive and confident self-regard and transferring that to your posture, physical attitude, responses, and actions. Empower yourself by knowing who you are and by striving to be better all the time with everything you do. Allow your posture to take on this mission and lift that chin up—even if you have baby drool on your shoulder! Once you evaluate your confidence and give it that needed injection of hope and strength, elegance will emanate from you.

To be elegant is to be compassionate and have empathy for others. With elegance, we work toward not judging how others may treat us. An example of using an elegant outlook might be when you go to the grocery store to pick up a few items for dinner, and at the register, you greet the cashier with a smile and she ignores you or barely looks up. An elegant reaction would be not to become insecure or take it personally; instead you continue to smile as you thank her for her help.

This means avoiding typical responses like "What's your problem?" or "I'm the customer and you should be nice to me." Elegance is not taking an awkward situation personally. There could be a multitude of reasons why she's not happy at that moment. It doesn't have to ruin your day.

Stay at Homework: Think back to moments when you held your composure and how that felt. Most likely, doing so boosted your self-esteem and confidence. Also consider those times when you lost your composure and regretted it. In your imagination change the outcome. How could you have maintained your dignity and taken the high road? Sometimes walking throughout our day with the intention to be elegant in our responses to others and circumstances can feel as if we are doing all the work. Remember that as we practice this attitude of elegance we are training ourselves to emanate assurance that no one will be able to deny. That air subtly speaks to them and they respond with kinder words and more respect. The key is to be consistent. As with any spiritual discipline, this one is strengthened each time we practice it.

Let's face it, ladies, when you're in the teller line at the bank and you have a baby on one hip and a toddler throwing a tantrum at your feet, it's hard to look elegant! That's why we encourage you to keep the basic elements of composure together even during the tougher times. Not because it will make you look better, but because it will make you *feel* better. By standing up straight, taking a deep breath, and keeping your dignity, you'll be more able to deal with the situation at hand. Elegance takes practice. We're going to give you some tangible tricks for mastering elegance on the outside so you can begin your elegant transformation within.

Stay at Homework: Check in with yourself several times a day and straighten that posture. Lift your rib cage out of your hips, put your shoulders back and your chin up! Remind yourself of the true meaning of elegance.

Stay at Homework: Grab your GAL Diary and record things you think about yourself as elegant. If you draw a blank, think hard. We promise that you have elegant talents and features. Go ahead and do a little bragging! Here are some suggestions to get you started. I

have good posture

have a warm, welcoming smile

am calm in stressful moments

understand how to make my family and friends feel good about
themselves

am a great hostess

understand colors, decor, and interior design

dress with style

am a positive person

am a great salesperson

know how to make a terrific chocolate cake

am a good dancer

As you can see, when we say "elegant" at MomsTown, we think of positive, powerful traits that add to your strength. Identifying these will help you feel more confident in a difficult situation. You have innate elegance; it's just a matter of noticing it and remembering it on a daily basis. As you begin to take note of your elegant traits, allow them to fuel your self-confidence and affect you in physical ways. Remember to have good posture and hold your head high, even in the most discouraging situations. We promise, it matters.

◆Hip Tip: Identify an elegant role model. MomsTown chose Jacqueline Kennedy Onassis as an inspiration. Jackie O was the embodiment of elegance—inside and out. The way she responded to life and tragedy was poised and elegant. She had great style. Think of someone who says elegance to you and how you might emulate that person in subtle ways. ◆

Authenticity

Be true. Be true to who you are and what you think. The MomsTown program strives to take you back to your most authentic, sure self.

To strengthen your own authenticity, be aware of any tendency you might have toward putting on airs and pretending to be something you are not. Notice the next time you feel you are not being authentic. Read the list below and be honest—do any of these apply to you?

- You get swept away with drama. You end up wasting a lot of time on silly or petty issues.

- You tend to get pulled into community initiatives you may not be interested in or concerned about.

- You volunteer for causes because you think you should, not because you want to.

- You attend social gatherings you feel you are supposed to rather than those you want to.

- You tend to give drawn-out, complicated reasons for why you can't commit to doing something.

- You have trouble simply saying no.

- You morph into the personality of others you are around. For example, if you're around a person who brags about him- or herself, you try to keep up by bragging about yourself. You're not secure in who you are.

Stay at Homework: Grab your diary and think of three things you've done in the past month that you didn't really want to do, that didn't appeal to the authentic you. How do you feel about those experiences?

Begin to notice when you are asked to participate in situations that don't appeal to your genuine sense of self. Seek out the beliefs and initiatives you stand for. You will know when you find them because when you begin working toward them, you will feel fulfilled. Perhaps you've always had a desire to work in a soup kitchen or work on an environmental cleanup project, but you have always been pulled into the bake sale or the knitting club instead. You dislike baking and can't knit a stitch, but you know you'd love helping gather support for a petition to save an endangered species. Figure out what it is that makes you feel authentically true to yourself, and then do it.

"I love volunteering at the blood drive and can't stand doing the school carnival, but always seem to do it when the other mothers pressure me into it. One year I realized I was letting myself be pulled into doing the carnival and missing out because the blood drive was the same week. I finally said no to the carnival and started doing the blood drive and it feels so much better," relates Cathy, a MomsTown member.

There is no prototype for authenticity because it is different with each person. What matters is that you are true to yourself. If you have some fixed idea about who you are, discard it right now. Authentic impulses and tastes can lead you in everything from your religious beliefs to your wardrobe. Do you identify authentically with Christianity or Buddhism, Birkenstocks or rhinestone heels? It is different for each person. Don't let yourself be pushed by the crowd—make your own path. Figuring out your authentic inner beliefs is part of getting it all. Getting it all begins when you admit who you are and what is important to you. Grab your diary and record what you think some of your authentic traits and beliefs are. What makes you feel the most like you? Forget what your friend, neighbor, or the model on TV enjoys. We're talking about the you who knows what your favorite foods are, has a particular talent that those closest to you know about, and has convictions and beliefs that truly mean something to you.

Stay at Homework: Grab your organizer and schedule in an authentic date with yourself for this week. This can be anything from attending a political rally to buying the yellow dress your friend said was too loud but you absolutely loved. Choose something that speaks to your taste or belief system, even if you've always denied yourself this authentic interest.

HUMILITY AND SISTERHOOD, THE MOMSTOWN WAY

"Life is a long lesson in humility," said James M. Barrie.

At MomsTown, we agree that all moms are in this together. Moms-Town operates on the premise that as moms we humbly recognize the universal truths that all other moms can relate to. This is what binds us. We are all doing the same thing: raising our children and living our own lives as we go. We all give birth, uncover motherly strength and perseverance, develop unbreakable emotional bonds with our children, wipe noses and bottoms, discipline and praise our children, and ultimately find we have a sisterhood of women who identify and understand our daily trials and triumphs.

The definition of being humble is the opposite of being proud or haughty, arrogant or aggressive. In the MomsTown program, we take that a step further. Keeping in mind the importance of what we share with so many other women makes us stronger and more effective as we move through our days, raise our children, and strive to get it all. Recognizing your place in the context of a community and exercising humility as you interact with other mothers and develop relationships that will support you means not judging women who do things differently. At MomsTown, and especially at this point in our program, we encourage you to remember this sisterhood. We ask you to recognize and exercise humility in doing so. Here are some definitions of humility the MomsTown way:

- Even though you are making dramatic changes in your life and are working toward getting it all, you should never look down on other mothers who might not appear to be doing the same.

- Outside of encouragement and invitations to do the Moms-Town program, watch out for any feelings of arrogance or condescension you might have toward mothers who are not trying to get it all.

- Recognize the difference between confidence and arrogance as you interact with other mothers and develop opinions about your authentic beliefs, parenting style, and what you want out of life.

- When you need support in your duties as a mother from someone other than your husband, other mothers can be the best answer. They understand what you go through from sunup to sundown.

- Exercising humility in your sisterhood with mothers will allow you to learn from other women you might otherwise have judged negatively and will put you in a better position to establish meaningful relationships.

The purpose of the above points is to make you more aware of your place in the community, locally, nationally, and through the MomsTown network. When you become aware of the whole sisterhood of moms, advantages and opportunities automatically open up to you. Just as business associates network to become more connected and do better business, moms benefit by networking to become stronger in their beliefs, strengths, parenting skills, and womanhood—or "Galhood," as we refer to it. Remind yourself regularly of this and become proactive in tapping into that mom universe, where you'll find unlimited support and raw Mom Power!

One of our moms, Beth, had great luck with playgroups and encourages others to try them. "Playgroups are great social activities to meet other moms and keep your kids entertained. Even if you're a one-car family, you can still organize a playgroup in your neighborhood by posting flyers and meeting at a park within walking distance. Play-groups allow moms to talk with other moms while their kids play with other kids. My oldest daughter started going to playgroups at eight months old, my youngest from two weeks, so age isn't a factor, either. Other variations of playgroups could be SAHM support networks, where moms meet at your house or a community center and do crafts, teach each other new things like scrapbooking, sewing, crocheting, or share recipes and timesavers. Kids are a wonderful conversation tool and they have an awesome way of getting even shy moms out of their shells."

Here are some ways to become an active organizer and seeker of other moms who can support, relate, and contribute to your efforts in getting it all! Mom Meetings are the way to get to know more moms and to have a working, functioning support system regularly with them.

- Check on the MomsTown Web site for a local chapter of MomsTown in your community. If there is none, consider start-ing one. Organize Mom Meetings under the umbrella of the MomsTown chapter. If you contact us at our Web site, we will give you more details.

- If you want to do it less officially, think of your closest mom friends and other moms you may know through school, church, the gym, or the neighborhood. Develop a list and get in touch with them about the times of day that work for them.

- Try to organize a MomsTown Meeting every week, every other week, or monthly, depending on what works for you.

• You can include the kids or not; take a vote with the other moms and see what the majority says.

• The MomsTown Meeting can be either a formal meeting, in which each mom brings up a challenge and a triumph she has faced in the past week, or an informal gathering where you simply get to know one another.

• Refreshments are fun, but don't put pressure on other moms to make something if you have it at someone's house. Allow the option for them to stop at the grocery store or bakery and pick up something already made. The less obligation and work that goes into attendance, the more moms will feel like joining.

• You can have the gathering in a neutral area, like a restaurant, playground, park, or beach, or you can take turns hosting the MomsTown Meeting.

• If you are uncomfortable with large groups, you can begin by regularly meeting with one or two mothers you know. The important part is getting to know other women who are moms, too. Gradually, as you get more comfortable with MomsTown Meetings, you can extend more invitations. In choosing the women you invite into your circle, try not to avoid certain moms because they seem like they have different styles, economic situations, or interests. You will be surprised at how much you have in common by virtue of motherhood alone.

• You don't have to call it the MomsTown Meeting if that doesn't suit you. Call it whatever you want—and even think of a name that fits your group. The key is to do it regularly and proactively seek out other moms.

Stay at Homework: This week begin a list of the moms you will invite to your MomsTown Meeting. Set a date. By the end of the week, extend the invitation or a save-the-date to at least two other mothers.

We had a group of MomsTown members who met every Monday night at their local bar and grill and had the best time! They called it Girls' Night, and their husbands and kids got used to making dinner for themselves or going out for pizza that particular night. They just came to accept that Mom would be out with the girls on that night. Gradually, the ladies got to know one another and looked forward to their Girls' Night because it became a place to talk about the adventures they had had as moms during the week and to get helpful input from other mothers. One member of the group, Jill, says of her times with the other women, "I could really talk about any aspect of my life from the funny stories of my husband changing the diaper to relating to the others about discipline techniques with my children and the isolation I felt as a mom, alone with a new baby and young three-year-old. The group became my solace. I began looking forward to Mondays—for the first time in my life!"

Another mother, Diana, who began a group in her neighborhood, started out with two attendees and now has eleven. "The list of friends I can call when I need advice about treating my child's fever or just to laugh with someone about something my husband or four-year-old said has grown considerably," she says. "I have a larger support group than I've ever had, and it gives me confidence and resources as I work through my daily schedule and work toward getting it all."

Most of us recognize through the pregnancy, the child's birth, and as the child grows, that there is a greater force at work. Regardless of your religious beliefs, we can all agree on this. Remember your first sonogram? You were amazed with the miracle of your inner self and your ability to give life. When you think back to that moment, know it was not only the seed of life of your child, but the seed of your future potential, inspiration, and power. All mothers share this experience, and a sisterhood emerges out of this universal role. This sisterhood of moms can be one of your greatest resources as you move toward your life goals.

Gratitude

If you are a mother, you automatically have a good deal to be grateful for: your children. As a living, breathing human being, you have your life to be grateful for. All of the countless things in between give you magical gifts on a regular basis. If you are not taking time to explore your gratitude and remind yourself on a regular basis of the things you are grateful for, you are not giving to your spiritual center and purpose, either.

The more you explore your inner gratitude for these things, the more confident you will feel, the more positive your attitude, and the more attention you will give those things or people you are thankful for. This may seem clichéd or hokey, but we've discovered that being aware of the things you appreciate is a meaningful centerpiece to your spiritual well-being and your daily happiness. You would be amazed how often we take our lives and our gifts for granted.

Stay at Homework: Grab your diary and list twenty things you are grateful for. Push yourself to notice things you don't necessarily consider during your Thanksgiving prayer.

Your child's health
Your health

Your inner passion (which we know you have if you are reading
   this book!)

Your husband

Your friends

Your community

Your plants that successfully grow in your garden

A person or stranger who unexpectedly went out of his or her
   way to do something nice for you recently

A good night's sleep

A home

Having the awareness to actively improve yourself and your self-
   worth

The list is endless. Make sure with your personal list you go from the large, obvious blessings to the often overlooked moments throughout your day—like tickling your child and hearing her giggle, the touch of your husband's hand, freedom to choose your life, and freedom to vote. Gratitude allows us to savor the moment—our lives, our children's lives, and the world around us as it is right now. You will never have that moment again.

Gratitude Gives You Power and Potential—and "GAL-itude"

MomsTown would like you to take the meaning of gratitude a step further. Go ahead and be grateful for what you have, but know that it's also okay to want more. That's right—you heard us. We give you permission to do both: be grateful but also want more. By virtue of being grateful, you draw positivity into your life. Wanting your life to be more fulfilling and wonderful, not only for yourself but for your family, does not mean you aren't grateful for what you have. Wanting success, more confidence, a better attitude, a better relationship with your husband, and pursuing your passions can all happen, even if you are grateful for what you have.

Take any guilt you have for wanting more and kiss it good-bye. That's "GAL-itude." In fact, wanting more is how you get it all. We've said it once and we'll say it again: This book is about you—not your children. You can be a thankful mother and still pursue your own life; that's what being a Gal is all about. Ward off that inner voice that says to you, "If you are trying to take care of yourself, you're selfish and do not have gratitude for your family." A Gal can do both, thank you very much! There is no rule that says you have to trade your quality of life for your children. You deserve everything you want (well, almost everything, except that daily chocolate sundae!).

Stay at Homework: One reason people don't get what they want out of life is because they aren't clear on what they desire. Earlier you recorded what you are grateful for. Now you are going to record what you will be grateful for in the future, once you've lived up to your dreams.

You were probably very clear about wanting to get married and have children. You may even have decided in advance how many children would be the ideal number. Take that same intention and get crystal clear on what more you want from your life. List the small material wants—such as a new sofa or pair of dynamite shoes—right on up to the outrageous "I want to be on *Survivor*" dreams. As the saying goes, "If you can conceive it and dream it, you can achieve it." MomsTown believes you must let your dreams live. List them here. Go ahead, you won't jinx things! Allow yourself to be grateful for what will happen if you only let yourself try. Here are some examples:

• You develop your interest in art and meet with a community art group that becomes active and raises money for a community art gallery.

- You become more fit, feel sexier, and start to feel great about your figure.

- You go out on romantic dates with your husband and come home and make love.

- You find yourself surrounded with friends who understand your values and support you in your success.

- You become a successfully published freelance writer.

- Your children grow up and look back on what a terrific inspiration you were to them through your hard work, pursuit of your dreams, and conviction in your beliefs.

- You sign up for a flamenco dance class to try out your new life.

- Instead of thinking your best years are behind you, reassure yourself your life experience has made you a savvy student and ready for life ahead.

- You are grateful to be healthy and decide to run a marathon or take tap lessons.

Achieving these goals is as simple as recognizing them and doing the work to make them a reality. Identify those things you would like to be grateful for in the future and release any fear that this forward-looking attitude reflects poorly on your appreciation for what you have now. Get comfortable with GAL-itude and celebrate it by taking action.

Stay at Homework: During your next session at your GAL sanctuary, take a moment to think about what you will be grateful for in the future and visualize the details of what that will be like. For example, you work hard in your dance class and can imagine dancing at your recital. Visualize every step of the routine executed flawlessly. Play that over and over in your mind. Allow yourself to assemble a whole scenario in which you are a phenomenal success. Imagine only the most positive outcome.

THE GAL VIRTUES

Courage

Getting a life can take courage. You are going to need to be brave about what you want, believe, and love. Think about it, you've already done one of the most courageous things a woman can possibly do: You have given life and have committed yourself to raising that child. Because of this, you know you have courage within you. Look inside and tap into it.

It takes courage to get over your big "buts." Big "buts" are habit forming, comforting, and very dangerous to your newfound Gal. Big "buts" go like this:

I would work out, **but** I just don't have time.

I would read that book, **but** I need to catch up on my soap opera.

I would get my hair done, **but** I can't fit it into my schedule.

I would clean out my closet, **but** I just can't bear to throw/give away my things.

I would take that art class, **but** what if I am really not all that talented?

Get over it! The big "but" is the enemy of the Gal, and the only way to get over it is to act with courage and discipline. Courage will shrink the big "but" until your confidence grows (and perhaps your pants size shrinks!).

Stay at Homework: Grab your diary and list ten of the things you typically preface with *but*. Think about some of the things you have always wanted to do but haven't done. This week, pick one of these things, focus on it, and do it. Get over one of your big "buts" with courage.

Maybe you are out of shape and you have always wanted to get outside and run a mile. You know it will be painful and you could possibly fail. Have the courage to try. Put one foot in front of the other and do it for yourself. The worst that can happen is you end up walking instead of running and can try again next time. You'll get further with courage than with doubt and fear, this we promise you.

It will take courage to admit to yourself what your deepest desires have always been. Have you always wanted to be an artist, writer, or yoga instructor? Here are some things to keep in mind when you hear yourself mention the word *but* in relation to something you'd like to do.

- You have an irrational fear that you will fail everyone, including yourself. The key here is that the fear is irrational and should not be taken seriously. It's about taking risks and accepting the outcome either way.

- You fear you will find out that you are not talented enough. You need to tell yourself that you are talented enough to begin and will get better with practice.

- You sabotage yourself by not trying. You deserve better than that—so try!

- Your negative, doubting inner self has control. Kick that bad attitude out of the driver's seat and shift your life into high gear. You deserve it.

- You cannot get a life without courage. You have come this far, and that proves that you have the courage necessary to get over a Big But.

The most exciting part about discovering the courage to pursue your dreams is that you already have that life-changing courage. All you have to do is find it and believe in yourself. You've been given the tools, now use them! Courage begets courage. The more you have overcome in the past, the more you are able to overcome in the future. It takes courage to follow the MomsTown program. To want it all is common, but to get it all takes uncommon conviction and commitment.

Stay at Homework: Listen to how you phrase sentences. Are you getting over your Big But or hiding behind it? In order to get it all, there can be no excuses.

If a mom makes a statement with the word *but* in it, she is discounting the first half of the sentence. For instance, "I want to work out, but I can't find the time." What she's really saying is "I don't want to work out and this is my excuse." Another example: "I would really like to go out with the girls, but I'm really tired." Ignore everything that follows the *but*.

One of our moms, Roxy, said of this exercise, "I couldn't believe how often I said *but* once I started to notice it. Every time I said it I paused and identified something I was struggling with. Most often, I felt a lot better when I figured out why I was making the excuse with *but* and used more proactive, positive language."

Stay at Homework: Grab your diary and make a list of what you have done in your life that took courage. You can say right away what we've already said—your children. We are willing to bet there are more than a few instances in your life when you've exhibited profound courage. Remember those times and how it felt. Go back to and find that courage and use it for your new goals.

Work Ethic

Labor will get you results in the MomsTown program. The piece of your spiritual balancing that will take hard work, sweat, and effort to get a life requires dedication. Spiritual labor means putting time into your workout, diary, schedule, friends, family, and life.

We have some good news: Labor doesn't have to be something you dread. It doesn't have to be soul-wrenchingly difficult. In fact, we believe labor can be rewarding. Labor can be fueled by passion and enthusiasm. If you have found your interests, desires, and passions, working these into the other dimensions of your life will invigorate you. Getting up in the morning and facing a day of engaged, passionate activities can be exciting. Perspective and attitude can change the way you see your own schedule.

As we said with courage, you know from your spiritual and physical experiences of child-bearing that you are capable of courage. We feel the same way about labor in the home, taking care of your kids, and working toward your passion. You are capable of it because you have been through it with your children during their birth—not just the physical labor of having children, but the heart and soul you invested in the very act.

Your experience as a mom should empower your devotion and ability to deal with labor. The routine of child care requires an enormous amount of work. Raising children takes dynamic, difficult schedules. If you can make it from sunup to sundown feeding, caring, cleaning, chiding, laughing, crying, flinching, hugging, and the million little things that go into being a mom—you can get a life!

We can't say it enough: Labor can be a wonderfully rewarding act. Goddesses do their share of sweating. Remember, you are not always a servant when you perform duties in your household. Your work ethic and your perception of yourself as a goddess rather than as a servant can transform the very act of labor. Here are some activities that require labor. Your very attitude about labor can change how enjoyable they are. Focus on enjoying them as you do them, rather than seeing them as routine, a burden, or a chore to get to an end result.

Cooking dinner for your family
Folding laundry
Bathing your children
Watering your plants
Cleaning out a cluttered space (closet, drawers, etc.)
Washing dishes
Tucking your children into bed at night

One of our moms, Janice, felt weighed down with the daily and weekly chores she did on behalf of her family. She noticed she was getting bitter and feeling unappreciated in her role as mom. "I felt I was missing out on something meaningful or important. Every time I did the laundry and put it away, there was another pile the next day. I thought to myself, how could I be accomplishing something meaningful while doing these chores? I love my husband and children and I wanted to stop the resentment that was building each time I prepared meals and started the soak cycle on the washer. One day, as I was feeling sorry for myself, knee-deep in socks, shorts, and towels to fold, I spied my three-year-old daughter's favorite pink dress. I had to smile because that is her favorite dress and the one she asked for every day. If it weren't clean she would be genuinely disappointed. On the days it was freshly washed, I would ask her if she wanted to wear it and she would beam and run to me to get dressed. In the laundry room I picked up that dress and smelled the fabric. I imagined how happy it makes her when she wears that dress. At that moment I realized I'm not just washing clothes, I'm creating comfort and warmth for my children. I took that feeling and extended it to cooking. That night as I prepared dinner I thought, 'I am nurturing my children's growth and contributing to their health while creating a space for the ritual of sharing a meal with those I love.' This approach genuinely changed my outlook on the labor I do in my household. It makes me a goddess and not a servant."

Janice's initial frustrations are not unusual. How often have you felt that cooking, cleaning, making beds, and picking up toys is a meaningless chore? When you feel this frustration, consider the deeper meaning of the role you play as a mother. Here are some things you can remember and think to yourself during your work at home:

- You are the nurturer.

- You set the emotional and physical tone of the household.

- Your children feel safe around you and derive comfort from your attention to their needs. Your husband does, too.

- It is an expression of love each time you do an act of service for another person.

- You're not just cooking breakfast or dinner, you're telling your loved ones you care about them and that they are important to you.

Moms are the great self-esteem builders. If you do an act begrudgingly, the message you send is that you may not care if your kids eat well and that what you do for your family feels like an infringement on what you really want to do. Find a place of honor and joy in labor. If you are putting work into our program, you will find yourself more fulfilled, less cranky, and less likely to feel frustrated by daily chores.

Stay at Homework: Grab your diary and take a moment to think about the kind of labor you went through when you gave birth to your children. Now, allow yourself to think about other forms of labor you have endured. Consider moments of your life in which you have worked harder than you have ever worked. List at least five of those instances. These didn't just take physical ability; it took spiritual devotion to the task at hand. If you have followed our advice on developing your passions and interests, you will find labor to be a productive means to a rewarding end. And as the above exercise suggests, labor does not have to be tedious, it can be rewarding and gratifying. Remember, the experience is controlled by your attitude.

Stay at Homework: During your next time in your sanctuary, focus on the role that labor plays in your life and allow yourself to reflect positively about that labor. Focus on enjoying the labor of your day. This has the power to change your entire outlook.

Self-discipline

Doing the MomsTown program requires self-discipline. Yes, we mean skipping dessert more often than not, bidding farewell to the drama of *Days of Our Lives,* and treating stress with exercise rather than a candy bar or a cocktail. We've had moms who have developed a strong sense of discipline by staying true to their goals and the steps of the program. The results have been profound. One of our Moms-Town members, Tracy, says, "When I stick to my workouts, my schedule, and spend time in my sanctuary, I feel so powerful. The very act of getting things done in a resolute, determined way makes me feel fantastic! It makes me feel that I can accomplish anything if I stick to the program."

Self-discipline involves following the guidelines you set for yourself, adhering to your schedule, and recognizing the parts of your life that require willpower. We believe self-discipline means avoiding those things we might mislabel as "options." Sometimes, when moms think of reasons not to do what they know they need to do, or what they have on their schedule, they label excuses as options. Here are some examples:

I could go work out or I could go have a nice big lunch.
I could go to my sanctuary or I could watch TV.
I could tackle that item on my Anti-Clutter list or I could watch
   Dora the Explorer with my daughter.
I could make a healthy dinner or we could go out for pizza.

Often our Big Buts allow us to have a few too many "options." Take a close look at these alternatives you give yourself and see what the outcome will be in your energy level and your sense of accomplishment. If you have a nice big lunch instead of tackling the gym—the item you might have originally scheduled on your list—how will you feel about yourself? Is the outcome better or worse than if you stick to your workout commitment? Pam says when she took the option of not working out away from her schedule she exercised consistently. When asked how she came to take away her not-working-out option she said, "I figured I don't have the option to not get out of bed in the morning, so why would I have the option to not exercise? If I made it a must-do, then it was automatically as much a part of my day as taking a shower, eating and sleeping and breathing. I treated a workout as essential to my health, well-being, and emotional state."

Stay at Homework: Grab your diary and copy the following list.

Must-Do's

1 Work out
2 Sanctuary
3 Anti-Clutter list
4 GAL Diary Duty
5 Time to read the newspaper

These are all tasks from our program. You can list two other tasks that you feel are Must-Do's or that are mentioned in our program. Now, underneath this list in your diary, write another list labeled "Excuses" and write an excuse you have thought of or used before for each of the above, using the corresponding numbers, as in this example.

Excuses

1 I would rather watch TV than work out.
2 I need to go shopping instead of spending time in my sanctuary.

After you've listed some of your favorite excuses, go down both lists and describe how you feel AFTER you've done each must-do.

Must Do's

1 Work out: I feel tired but good and proud of myself.
2 Sanctuary: I feel better about the way the hectic morning was and how the afternoon can be. I feel more calm and able to get through my day . . .

Excuses

1 Watch TV instead of work out: Feel guilty I didn't work out, and end up confessing to anyone who will listen that I skipped it.
2 Shopping instead of sanctuary: Found myself frazzled by mid-afternoon, rather than focused and calm.

By closely examining the effects that our actions have on our sense of self and well-being, we can make better choices and recognize many of our "options" as excuses. In this way, self-discipline is directly related to our attitude and our perception of ourselves. Self-discipline is one of the major keys to your success. Self-discipline and doing those things necessary for a quality life builds self-esteem.

THE TRUTH TEST

Sometimes it can be challenging to recognize some of the patterns and habits you have formed. You may be a pro at disguising your excuses as options. Next time you feel yourself weighing options and you're not sure if they are really excuses, ask yourself the following:

• How will this action affect my progress toward getting it all?

• How will I feel after I finish doing this activity?

- How does this activity affect my confidence, self-image, and attitude?

- After I'm finished, will I feel proud? Calm and clear? Guilty and regretful? Like a fabulous Gal, or a "regular ol' SAHM"?

Many of our excuses we use regularly can be disguised as options or alternatives and seem just all around easier in the beginning. In the end, how do the activities you do in your day affect the inner you? How do they affect your authenticity, clarity, and goals? That is what you must ask yourself when you are at the crossroads between the Stair-Master and a quesadilla at your favorite restaurant. These are the instances when self-discipline has an effect on who you are and how you feel about yourself.

Pinpoint what your weaknesses are. Perhaps you're very good at working out when you have it on your calendar, but can't seem to make time to get organized or clean out your pantry or closet. Every time you arrange to do it, something else comes up. Think for a moment, and see where in your life you need self-discipline. Is it

- making time for your own hobbies?

- working out?

- organizing your office?

- meeting a friend for lunch?

- having date night with your husband?

• making time to read your favorite magazine?

• making sure you don't eat junk food?

• making sure you don't watch TV so often?

You know where you need to cut out options that interfere with self-discipline.

Stay at Homework: Make a list of five areas you want to improve your self-discipline in. During the rest of the program when you get stuck in a seemingly tough decision in each of those areas, remember our Truth Test.

Self-discipline is non-negotiable. Your sanity and your well-being demand setting boundaries and sticking to the things you know you need to do. You owe it to yourself and the Gal inside you!

Forgiving

"Once a woman has forgiven her man, she must not reheat his sins for breakfast," said Marlene Dietrich.

We are all human. While we at MomsTown stress self-discipline, we also know it's okay to give yourself a break every once in a while. Let's face it: You've got commitments ranging from finger painting to potty training to your own weight training! Considering we always say "everything in moderation," the way to balance self-discipline is with forgiveness. Forgiving yourself is key to keeping a positive attitude and not getting bogged down by things you could've, should've, would've done differently.

Forgiveness allows us to get through our days. We need forgiveness for our children, husbands, friends, and family when they push our buttons. Forgiveness helps us not take everything so seriously. We have all thrown a piece of Tupperware across the room in frustration. We are allowed. Most important, we need to forgive ourselves. Here are some basic reasons to practice forgiveness:

- Not forgiving yourself takes valuable energy from your day and your momentum.

- Not forgiving your kids, husband, mother, or friends is emotionally draining. Why waste a moment longer harboring negative feelings toward a person you love?

- If you're holding a grudge toward someone you don't know very well (e.g., that snobby, condescending mom at your son's preschool), try to think ahead to the future—will you really care about this situation in a couple of years? The answer is almost always no. So stop wasting time, energy, and emotion now.

- Holding a grudge against your mother-in-law because she tries to tell you what color to paint your kitchen, how to raise your children, and what kind of haircut to get strains family relationships. (Well, okay, it's all right to hold a grudge for a day or so with this one, but don't let it take over your life!)

Watch yourself and be aware of grudges you might be holding against members of your family, neighbors, friends, or other mothers. Realize that your power to let go of these grudges will only strengthen you, while holding on to them will drag you down. Choosing your battles will allow you more energy to fight the ones that matter, and not waste energy on the ones that don't.

Forgiving ourselves means giving ourselves a break. All moms have similar regrets, fears, self-doubt, and guilt. Forgiving brings us power and perspective. It is one of the most important balancers we are given. With the power of forgiveness comes humor, laughing at others (and ourselves) rather than allowing anger and frustration to rule the day. Allow yourself to ask, "Is my head spinning? Am I out of control?" Capture a comical, cartoon-like image of yourself that allows you to giggle, and file it away. Pull it out when you find yourself at an extreme point of frustration; think of a comic image of yourself and forgive whatever has made you angry. Laugh about it.

Stay at Homework: Take a moment to think about any grudges that are dragging you down. Find strength within yourself and work on forgiving. Grab your diary and write a description of yourself at your most angry, but in a comical light. Think of how funny you must look! Make sure it makes you giggle and file it away. Think about this when you find yourself extremely frustrated, and forgive with humor. Next time your son or daughter purposefully pushes your buttons, your husband forgets to pick up the ONLY thing you asked him to get at the grocery, or your in-laws criticize your recipe for your special homemade meatloaf, take a moment to think rather than just reacting. You'll be glad you did.

THREE CORE VALUES OF GAL-DOM

Reminding ourselves of our core values takes diligence. All of these values demand maintenance in your daily awareness. If you want your children to have these qualities, you have to remain faithful to them as well.

Integrity: Be honest with yourself. Many people use small and large lies on a regular basis and avoid facing truths that might force them to change. Don't be the queen of denial as you evaluate what you want and do not want in your life.

Loyalty: Being loyal to yourself will bring loyalty in all other areas of your life. Everything we cover in this book requires loyalty to yourself and your life. Loyalty to your beliefs, schedule, passions, and self-discipline will bring happiness.

Respect: When you respect yourself, you find respect for others. SAHMs must learn to respect their decision to stay at home or no one else will. Being a Gal means respecting what you stand for as a SAHM as well as respecting the identity you have outside of being a mom.

BREATHE

It's essential to take time out of the day, not only in your sanctuary, but anywhere you might be, if only five minutes, to breathe, clear your mind, and focus. What we cover in this chapter takes a process. It won't happen all at once. Find a time of day, maybe right before you go to bed, when you get up, when the kids are taking a nap, or before you pick them up at school, where you can regularly take five to ten minutes. If you want to meditate, this is the perfect place to start. We believe traditional meditation is just one way to connect with your inner spiritual strength. For those who are not drawn to meditation, just breathe. Just taking a moment to be, to breathe every day, is enough. You owe it to yourself, and you will find yourself a lot saner and clearer.

WEEK 6 SUMMARY

1. Find a place to set up your GAL Sanctuary and go to it every day—try for at least fifteen minutes. Collect your sanctuary accessories and remember to pamper yourself! In one of your GAL Sanctuary sessions, focus on the things that you are grateful for and then focus on what you will be grateful for in the future after you achieve your goals. Imagine the details of achieving your goals.

2. Remember your elegant GAL-itude and allow that to fuel your confidence and your posture throughout the day.

3. Notice when you get pulled away from your authentic self and find yourself doing things your heart isn't in.

4. Go on an authentic date with yourself (and if you need to, you're allowed to bring the kids).

5. Attend or organize a MomsTown Meeting and invite moms.

6. Remember that self-discipline will not only lead you to finishing tasks but also will boost your self-esteem, confidence, and success.

7. Let go of a grudge you're holding and don't be so quick to anger. Forgiveness is a gift you give yourself.

8. Remember your comical picture of yourself. Visualize it the next time you are frustrated or angry.

9. Breathe consciously every day.

WEEK 7: THE MOMSTOWN ALARM CLOCK: IT'S TIME TO WAKE UP YOUR DREAMS

Sometimes as moms we feel as if we know our duties and our job in our homes so well we could go through our daily routines in our sleep. After you've changed your four hundredth diaper, folded fifteen hundred loads of laundry, made three hundred trips to the grocery store, made two thousand, six hundred and eighty-two peanut-butter-and-jelly sandwiches, and picked up eighteen thousand toys, you've got the routine down. Sometimes the daily monotony of chores can lull you into complacency, a foggy dreamlike state where one day melds into the next. At MomsTown we're going to show you how to wake up.

This week we will help you find that spark to liven up your energy and routine. The number one question we're asked by moms is "How do you do it all? How do you take care of the family, host a radio show, write a book, and put dinner on the table every night?" We are able to do it because we have incorporated our passions and interests into our daily responsibilities. Teaching moms to get it all and how to improve their lives and find their passions just happens to be our dream and our passion. Having success doing what we love keeps us going, through the chores and diaper changes. Developing a program to help moms live their lives to the fullest makes our days a lot more exciting than the "same ol' routine." You will find that the key to your success lies in finding your passion and incorporating it into your life. By identifying and articulating your dream, you are taking your first step toward a richer, fuller, and more adventure-filled daily life. This week, we'll walk you through exercises and tips to figure out what passions will liven up your life.

These are many obvious examples of famous moms who have continued to develop their passions. Courteney Cox Arquette, mother of one, is actively continuing her acting career and is passionate about interior design. Kelly Ripa, mother of three, added television talk shows and sitcoms to her acting repertoire because she loves her work so much. We all know Madonna, who is a mother of two, has pursued all kinds of passions, including singing, performance art, acting, yoga, writing children's books, and seeking spiritual enlightenment.

Once you begin to uncover your passion and pursue it in large and small ways, your passion can become addictive. Each creative encounter deepens your desire to have more in your life. Creativity and dreams are not just for the rich and famous, they are for you—the everyday mom. In fact, creativity helps you realize that there is no such thing as an everyday mom; you are a mom who is so much more.

You may think that you don't have a creative bone in your body. We can assure you that this is not true. Like any kind of activity, creativity gets easier the more you practice it. Creativity can take so many forms. This week we will find what form your creativity will take.

In talking about passion, we don't dismiss your devotion and passion for your children and family. We recognize moms love their responsibilities and caring for their loved ones. At MomsTown, we applaud your devotion to your mom duties but urge you to explore your creative power to do more. This week we will tap into it and guide you as you take your creativity a step further, the next step toward getting it all.

THINK OUTSIDE THE SAHM BOX

Take a moment and imagine that you are inside a box. The four walls around you are your traditional routine, everyone else's expectations, and the feelings you have when you feel worn out and stressed. Those things in your life that make you feel trapped—that stunt your potential growth and passions—form the walls of what we call the SAHM box. As a sandbox keeps sand from spilling out, this box keeps the grains and the beginning of your creativity and dreams confined.

Stay inside this imaginary place in your mind and imagine all of the things you want to explore outside the box. Perhaps people are actually taking belly-dancing lessons out there somewhere. Maybe you can visualize yourself taking a workshop on public speaking. Try to see yourself doing something interesting, fun, and exciting. This week we are going to take you outside the SAHM box.

Moms tend to get focused on the practical, basic things, such as laundry, preparing meals, the family finances, and playing referee. This is normal, and we do need to be focused on these things. But you are capable of focusing on other interests without sacrificing your role as mom.

Stay at Homework: Get your kids' crayons, watercolors, or colored pencils and draw a picture. You can do this while your kids are coloring theirs. Participate in art time. Draw a picture or a snapshot of what your dream life would be like. Give the picture attention and imagine yourself in it. What types of things do you see surrounding you in the future, in your dream scenario?

Engage your sensory recall. What were your favorite smells and tastes when you were a child? List them. Now list your favorite smells and tastes as an adult. What colors do you see? Are they vibrant reds and yellows, or darker browns and blacks?

TAKE YOUR GAL ON AN ADVENTURE

Do you have an unlived-in adventure in you? Of course! Chances are you have more than one. And if you can't think of any, you're not thinking hard enough. The ordinary SAHM may not dream of adventure, but the Gal surely does. Adventures come in all shapes and packages. The determining factor for calling it an adventure is that it takes you out of your daily routine. The definition of *adventure,* as most of us know it, is the undertaking of some type of risk, or maybe going head-first into the unknown.

At MomsTown, we have found adventure assists in the development of the Gal. For the Gal to materialize, she needs to take risks, to have an exciting or remarkable experience to call her own. This can happen in very simple, everyday ways. Just venturing out of the daily routine and typical SAHM goals is a risk and adventure. Make it simple at first and build from there. Create your own adventure that speaks to your inner wishes for excitement and confidence. Some adventures our MomsTown members are interested in taking are:

Taking a pottery class
Learning public speaking
Taking a voice lesson
Taking dance lessons
Running a 10K race
Planning a safari vacation for the family

Learning to surf

Taking a family road trip

Hiking with a community hiking club

Climbing Mount Everest

Taking dance lessons with your husband

Joining a book club

Starting a garden

Throwing a dinner party

Trying a different drink at dinner

Reading a new book genre

Painting a wall in your house a color you've always loved

Going to a cocktail party where you know only one person (or
no one at all!)

As you can see, these can be major or minor, physical, cultural, or mental adventures. Anything that deviates from your typical habits will reawaken your spirit, imagination, and sense of adventure. Watch out for anxiety and fear of a different routine or goal. Remember: This is just an adventure! Let yourself feel excitement, not fear.

One of our moms, Erin, had a fear of the ocean. Although Erin knew how to swim, the vastness of the ocean, and the waves and currents, was terrifying for her. But wouldn't you know, Erin married a sailor. Her husband loved to race Hobie Cats. Erin had a choice: to be left on the shore or to confront what terrified her most. She finally decided to strap on a life jacket and headed out onto the open water. The first time out on the water, Erin broke out into a sweat. She could feel her heart beating through the life vest. But each time she went out, it became easier, as she focused on the competition of racing boats and being a member of the enthusiastic crew. Erin is proud that she didn't let her overwhelming fear sideline her, though sailing is still not her favorite hobby. She doesn't have to hear about the excitement and thrill of the race secondhand—she lives it. And living fully is more important than living fearfully.

Stay at Homework: Grab your diary and answer the following questions. Do you have a fear that you can overcome? What is it? How could you face that fear head-on? What could you focus on to diminish your fear? For example, Erin focused on the deck of the boat. She also focused on the competition and on someone whose experience she could trust.

Stay at Homework: Take a moment and write down some adventures you've always wanted to have. Put the wheels in motion to do them. Go on one adventure this week.

DREAM AND DARE TO IMAGINE

Throughout the program we've been concentrating on the importance of discovering your passions and interests. During each step, we want you to push yourself a bit further. This week we want you to focus on allowing your inner Gal to speak out. Allow anything that comes to mind to come out during these exercises. The more honest you become with yourself, the closer you are to obtaining your dreams.

Stay at Homework: Grab your diary and write down some of your dreams. Think about what your answers are to some of the following questions.

- What is your dream vacation? Try to focus on the details, not just the place. What would you have for dinner? To drink? To wear? Who would you meet?

• What is your dream date with your husband? Be impractical! Maybe it's going somewhere out of the country on a private jet, or a roller-coaster ride ending in a seductive rendezvous behind the cotton candy stand.

• If you could be a movie star, who would you be? Why? Is it because they get to wear expensive, fancy dresses, or work on a movie set? Maybe you need a dress made for a movie star and a date you can wear it on.

• If you could be a rock star, who would you be? Why? Would you like to unleash your inner Gal onstage in front of thousands? Or have permission to wear your hair in a crazy style or color? Perhaps there is a variation for everyday wear that you can try. Do some research and find out.

• If you had to wear one color from head to toe for a whole week, what would it be? Buy more clothes in this color and wear them! Mary's favorite color is pink, and sometimes she wears it from head to toe.

• What was your favorite piece of clothing when you were a girl? If you can't remember, call your mom and ask. Was it a tutu, cowboy boots, a baseball cap, or a tiara? Does this remind you of a piece of your personal style you can incorporate into your wardrobe?

• If you could drive any car, what kind would it be? Go out and test-drive that car. Why not?

- What were your favorite games to play when you were a girl? Maybe you played house, hide-and-seek, Monopoly, or attack of the aliens. Try to remember and then play at least one of these games with your kids this week.

GAL Dream File

You can get a good idea of some of your passions and dreams by doing research. Have you ever done research on your dreams? It can be fun and entertaining. You can discover dreams you never knew you had. One of the ways to do this is to compile an ongoing dream file.

Gather at least a half dozen magazines, books, and newspapers. If you need to go to Barnes & Noble or Borders and buy more magazines, go for it. Keep in mind they don't have to be new magazines or newspapers.

- Grab scissors, photocopy paper or construction paper, and glue or tape.

- The kids can do their dream files along with you if they're the right age.

- Set up somewhere that has enough room to spread out, maybe the kitchen or dining room table, or the living room floor.

- Take time to look through magazines, books, and newspapers. Find pictures and quotes that inspire you and cut them out.

- Paste or tape them onto sheets of paper.

- Get a folder—any kind will do—and give it a fun label like "Heather's Dream Items." Or if you'd rather, post your pictures on a corkboard.

- Keep adding to this file or dream board whenever you see something that inspires you.

Simply forcing yourself to seek out items or quotes that make you feel great and inspire you toward greatness can elevate your mood and give you a context in which to discover dreams to add to your dream list. Don't let your current money situation hinder your dreams. You might look for a(n)

vibrant color scheme or decorating technique for your house

special way to arrange your bedroom (canopy bed, type of art, etc.)

outfit you wish you could wear

pair of shoes you wish you had

place you would like to visit

color that makes you feel good

picture of people that makes you feel joy

quote from your favorite author

title of a book that changed your life

design that makes you feel soulful, sad, or thrilled

fortune-cookie note you got on a date with your husband or children

It is hard to articulate what images and words will speak to each person's passions. The inherent uniqueness in everyone makes it impossible for us to say what your passion might be. But we can advise that sometimes, if you cannot articulate it, you must just see it and feel it. Allow yourself to be open to these dreams and hopes.

Another tool for inspiration is a quote frame. This is a picture frame you can keep on your desk or nightstand or in your kitchen that holds your favorite quote of the week, month, or year. Change it whenever you find a new quote to go in it. The quote should inspire and remind you. Perhaps it is from a famous person, a friend, or something you came up with in your diary.

These are just a few ideas to bring your passion and imagination to the forefront of your daily routine. If you allow yourself, you will invent other ways to be creative and let your imagination soar. Be open to them, and when they come to you, write them down in your GAL Diary and share them with a buddy. We all need reminders to let our inner Gal's imagination breathe.

Your Crazy Dream

We've done this program with other moms and we've had diverse reactions to different aspects of it—all good—but one thing that's uniform, and a sure bet with every mom, is that every person has a crazy dream. Sometimes we are able to admit things if we dismiss them as crazy. Chances are, it's not even that crazy. When asked what their dreams are, many moms have answers similar to our mom Bonnie's: "I would like to take my businesses to a higher level, and then have time and extra money to do other things. I'd love to learn how to play guitar, take some classes, get involved volunteering for a social cause."

We'd like you to admit your crazy dream.

Stay at Homework: Grab your diary and list your favorite dream (famous sculptor, musician, screenwriter, artist, amazing gardener, etc.).

+ Describe it in detail.

+ List what you would like about this dream coming true.

+ Choose someone who has made his or her dreams come true to be your inspiration.

+ Figure out a way to make your dream happen—even if you think it's crazy!

+ Figure out what you will do in the next four to five years to make this happen.

+ Now work backward and figure out what you can do in the next year, nine months, six months, month, week, and today.

+ Choose one thing to do today toward that dream.

+ Stop referring to it in your mind as a "crazy" dream. Let it just be okay that you have that dream.

We've had the most remarkable results with women who have done this. One mom, Allison, wanted to begin painting and went out and bought paint supplies the first day we started the program with her. The next six months she focused on painting each day whenever she had a free moment. Allison slowly gained enough confidence in her skill to approach a local coffeehouse that had a small gallery of local artists displaying their art. She sold her first painting within a month and now she's working on placing her art in other galleries. She has now been featured nationally in magazines and is considered one of the great local talents in her area. Allison says of her experience, "I really just had to admit I wanted to paint and I had always wanted to paint. As soon as I did that and started developing a long-term and a short-term plan to make it happen, things just kind of fell into place. I am so grateful I took the beginning steps. My life is richer and fuller because of it." We hear stories like this a lot from mothers. Often when we identify what it is we want to do, things will start working for us in ways we hadn't imagined.

Most of us who have been pregnant know the store A Pea in the Pod. The owner of this business identified what she wanted and began putting things in place to get it. She began selling only one blue suit for working pregnant moms—one suit and one very big dream for a chain of boutiques across the country. And now she has developed some of the most successful clothing lines around. Her dream came true by realizing it and working toward it.

Realizing Your Dream Goal Every Day

Now that you have done some work to figure out what your dream is, let's practice focusing that dream every day. Here are some ways to do that.

Create a GAL Mantra that says your name and what you want to be after it. This is similar to a name tag. Insert your name and then your dream—for example, "Sally Lawson, author." With this name tag, establish your new identity.

Post it on your refrigerator.

Use it as a bookmark or page mark for your diary by adding your name tag to a folded piece of paper or cardboard.

Put it in your GAL Sanctuary.

Repeat your name tag aloud whenever you see it.

Use your name tag as a screen saver.

Use it as a page marker in your organizer.

Stay at Homework: Do two of the above, or your own variation, this week. The more real you make this dream for yourself, the more real the dream will actually become. Begin to allow this dream to take shape and let yourself own this identity. The result is up to you.

Stay at Homework: Grab your diary and write an entry about your new identity. Begin it with [your name], [your dream identity]. Talk about yourself positively and be as honest as you would with a friend who is beginning a journey you are happy she is taking. Nurture yourself with at least three compliments in this entry.

Here is an example one of our moms, Larissa, volunteered from her GAL diary. "I am Larissa, guitarist. I want to be a talented, trained musician. I enjoy music and believe I have a knack for rhythm and melody. I am musically inclined and can learn to play the guitar if I put my mind to it."

Use this template if you need to:

I am _____, _____. I am talented and very good at _____. I enjoy _____ and will be successful at _____. I will spend time developing my dream so I can feel confident and able to _____ in the next _____. My special talents include _____. I will excel at _____ if I put work into it and put my mind to it. I am inherently creative and talented and can do whatever I want.

Using your GAL Diary to write down your goals is a great way to keep them at the forefront of your mind. One of our moms, Tracy, said the most helpful thing she does is to keep "writing down goals. Actually detailing the way I want my life to be and then taking baby steps to get me there."

Fear and Faith

There are all sorts of things that hold us back when we consider our dreams. One of the most powerful is fear. Fear feeds on any situation in which you are venturing out of your comfort zone and into a new part of your life.

One of our MomsTown members, Olivia, had a dream to write. "I wanted to take a creative writing course and was so scared!" she says. "I was worried that I would be terrible and it would be humiliating and embarrassing. I had to have faith that I could do it even though my fear tried to talk me out of it. I can remember the first time as a class we had to read work aloud. I was so afraid. And once I finished, I had praise from so many people in the class! I couldn't believe it. From that point on, I decided to trust my faith in my dreams rather than my fear. All I had to do was act against my fear. I now see that connection. It has enabled me to do so much."

Stay at Homework: You can do this, too. We've helped countless women overcome their fears on their way to achieving their dreams. Here are a few questions to answer as you begin to put things in motion toward your dream. Consider the examples that follow each question.

What are you afraid of?

- Rejection
- Embarrassment
- Failure
- Getting what you want

Think about the above carefully and face your inner self. Grab your diary and write down the fears that you have. Why do you think these particular fears are there?

What actions or feelings are perpetuated by these fears?

* Sabotaging yourself and your future successes
* Staying in your comfort zone
* Laziness and procrastination
* Relying on excuses rather than faith
* Feelings that you are not worth it and are not talented
* Guilt over thinking about goals beyond raising your kids

Grab your diary and identify which of the above actions or feelings, as well as any others not listed, apply to you. Figure out what techniques you tend to use to avoid starting on your journey toward getting it all.

How can you overcome your fears?

* By taking risks and adventures and telling yourself you have faith.

* By not listening to people you don't admire and who don't support the better parts of you.

* By doing something every single day, even if it is repeating your GAL Mantra and sticking to your schedule and workouts, in order to get closer to the person you want to be.

* By not giving in to procrastination, indifference, or depression.

- By thinking about the positive outcome rather than the negative possibilities.

- By having faith that you are worth it and you're one heck of a Gal!

Our client Jeanne had always wanted to be a public speaker. She often spoke up at community meetings and had a knack for conveying ideas in a passionate, convincing way. When she considered doing it professionally, though, she became paralyzed with fear. She was afraid that if she tried she would fail. With the support of her family and fellow moms, she began to take public speaking classes in spite of all of her doubts and fears. At the end of the class, she did her final project, which was to prepare a speech and present it at the next community meeting. She was wonderful and everyone applauded her.

"The hardest thing to do was to sign up for the class," she says. "I was really scared that it would be horrible and everyone would laugh at me. As I worked toward doing homework for the class and preparing my final speech, my fears didn't go away, but they became less and less of the central focus. The best part was when I gave my final speech and my four-year-old came up to me and said, 'Mom, you were awesome!'"

On the MomsTown program, we don't guarantee that your fears will disappear, but we do promise that once you put faith in your vision and take action toward your dreams, they will become less daunting. Developing faith in yourself comes from repeatedly working toward your goal, taking action when you feel fear, and reminding yourself on a regular basis that you can do it.

The MomsTown Dream Log

In order to help you prioritize your plan for achieving your dream, this week we would like you to start a MomsTown Dream Log. This will be where you document and plan your next moves in the journey toward your dream. This activity can be done with the kids during their drawing/coloring time. You can use their supplies as they work on their art.

- Get two to five sheets of notebook or copy paper, more if you like to write a lot.

- Raid your kids' school supplies. Find a ruler and color markers, pens, or crayons.

- Write your dream identity from the previous exercise at the top of the first sheet of paper. It should have your name and your dream identity—for example, "Diane Smith, ballet dancer." Divide sheets of paper into a total of six sections with lines going across. Label them "Week 1" through "Week 6." Within each section make a subsection labeled "Goal" and "Action Taken." Make the sections large enough so that you have room to put what you would like to accomplish that week and what you actually did accomplish that week.

- Begin budgeting what actions you will apply toward achieving your dream each week of the next six weeks.

- Try not to overestimate, but be positive and upbeat about what you think you can achieve.

- Keep your MomsTown Dream Log somewhere safe. You are the only person who needs to see it.

- If you have an especially close relationship with your buddy, you may want to help each other stay on track by shaping your Dream Logs.

- Celebrate when you reach the end of your six weeks. Go out to dinner with the family or your buddy.

- Make another six-week Dream Log after you finish the first. You can only build from this point on!

Here is a sample of one MomsTown client's Dream Log.

Sandy White, photographer

Week 1
Goal: Do research on camera types.
Action taken: Found camera that suits the types of photos I like to take.

Week 2
Goal: Do research on classes to take in beginning photography.
Action taken: Went to stores, looked online, and talked to community photographers. Finally found class at the community college that meets twice a week and need to work out times with husband and babysitter.

Week 3
Goal: Start class.

Action taken: Worked out schedule with babysitter and husband for the first few weeks of class. I love class—it's so fun!

Week 4

Goal: Begin experimenting with camera.

Action taken: Took some great shots of the kids in the yard.

Week 5

Goal: Aggressively shooting rolls of film

Action taken: Have decided on a "nature" theme and have already taken thirty pictures of a national park while on vacation.

Week 6

Goal: Set up my own darkroom at home.

Action taken: A few people in my photography class showed me how to use my spare bathroom as a darkroom. I've arranged it so that no light gets in. Next week I will develop my first roll of pictures there. I'm so excited!

Achieving your dreams is a matter of putting one foot in front of the other and taking the necessary steps to accomplish them. As you progress, write us at MomsTown and let us know where you are with your Dream Log. We want to hear how things are going and we will give you that extra boost of support whenever you need it. We think you'll find a Dream Log is the perfect way to help yourself define in easy step-by-step ways what you are doing on a regular basis to think outside the SAHM box!

Keep the atmosphere in your home lively and inspiring. As you go through your day, remember that you don't have to be a mature, composed mom all of the time. Doing little things to relax and let your hair down can do wonders for your stress level—and your kids will enjoy it, too. It's good for them to see you more relaxed and lighthearted.

• Music is a great way to instantly change the mood of your house. Take time out of chores to dance. One of our moms, Denise, gave this advice: "Music really helps. Sometimes I have to force myself to put it on, but once I do, my children and I just get a little pep in our step. They love to watch me sing and dance around, too. It just brings a little levity to any situation and serves as sort of a 'restart.'" Go for music that creates a good mood and atmosphere in your house. Ask your kids to help you pick it out.

• Hang art throughout your house that makes you feel inspired and creative. You don't have to spend a lot of money to do this—you can make your own if you like! The cost of art is not what's important, it's how it makes you feel.

• Keep fresh flowers in your house. Again, these don't have to be the expensive, exotic kind. You will feel especially inspired if they are from your own yard or new garden!

SOCIALIZING YOUR PASSION: DO THE HUSTLE!

Just as we advocate putting action into obtaining your dreams, we believe a great deal of progress can happen if you make yourself available for social networking. One of our moms, Teresa, had the dream of being an interior designer. She subscribed to magazines and researched new trends on the Internet, but still felt she didn't know how to pursue her dream in a direct, aggressive way. One day she decided to accept an invitation to a party from neighbors she did not know very well. She was making an effort to get out more and decided it couldn't hurt to meet more people in her area. That night she met a man who was looking for an assistant for his interior design business. She was able to talk about the newest trends in interior design thanks to her research, and he asked her to work for him. He said she could work part time with flexible hours, considering she had three children. After a year or two, she felt confident enough to open her own studio with her own hours organized around when her kids were in school. She is now a successful interior designer.

Teresa says of the experience, "All it took was putting myself out there, in contact with people I might not normally meet. A year prior, I may not have accepted that party invite. After making the effort to learn about the interior design industry, I knew enough to strike up a conversation that launched my new business. It was just a matter of taking one step at a time. Things just seem to fall into place when you decide what you want."

We believe it's worth putting yourself out there to meet new people whenever you can. Socialize and be proactive. And even if you don't meet the person who can help your dreams come true, your life will be richer, with more friends and acquaintances. Remember that rarely do you attend a new event without learning something. Accept invitations to functions that sound interesting or unusual, including:

Community functions
Art shows
Music shows
Readings
Dinner parties
Host dinner parties
Dance lessons with your husband

If you are dreading going to something, resort to the one drink/half hour rule. Tell yourself you'll stay for only one drink or a half hour, whichever comes first; nine times out of ten, you'll stay longer and be glad you did. Sometimes we just need to feel the commitment is not overwhelming in order to get out the door.

Don't use your kids as an excuse not to attend a community function. Depending on your kids' ages, you can take them almost anywhere, unless the invitation is clearly for adults only. MomsTown etiquette says so! If you're unsure, ask if the kids are welcome and be frank about it. There are so many community activities that are kid-friendly; you can be sociable with your kids.

Getting out and being sociable can change your perspective and fuel your passion. It can put you in touch with your future best friend or inspiration. It can make your dreams come true. As we said above, a lot of SAHMs bring their kids along. One mom, Tracey, says of her outings, "I don't have problems focusing on my interests outside my daughter right now. We [my husband and I] just strap her into her car seat and bring her along for the ride. We started doing that right away. My first solo outing with her was when she was eight days old. I took her to a cocktail reception celebrating a friend's engagement. My husband was taking graduate classes and could not be there, but I was not going to miss it. She has adapted quite well to our breakneck pace."

And don't forget: Social engagements are a great opportunity for you to show off that new figure your regular workouts have contributed to! Not to mention they're the perfect place to share your new passion and extend yourself to new people.

The GAL Hostess

You don't have to think about socializing as just attending other people's functions. You can be an active, assertive GAL hostess. Throwing a dinner or cocktail party and inviting an eclectic group of people can be a huge amount of fun and can put you in touch with new people. Don't let the idea of entertaining overwhelm you; you don't have to offer a full five-course meal to have a party. Entertaining can be an empowering way to socialize, boosting your confidence as you network yourself out of the SAHM box. Keep it as simple as it needs to be to work with your busy schedule—the atmosphere will take care of itself. Here are some tips:

- Potluck can be a lifesaver! Ask each guest to bring a dish or an appetizer. To make it more fun, you can tell everyone there will be a vote for the best dish—with a prize, naturally!

- Keep it simple. You don't have to serve dinner. You can do heavy appetizers and tell people ahead of time that you're just doing appetizers and drinks.

- Have a dessert party. It's so much easier, and people will eat before they come.

- Barbecues are another way to simplify. Let your husband and all the other guys take over the main course. All you have to make is the veggies and the potato salad.

- Be adventurous with your invites. Invite people you may not know that well. Or ask guests to invite friends you don't know well.

Throwing a party is an empowering way to follow up after you meet new people at other events. Don't underestimate the power of meeting people and being sociable. It can help you bring your closeted dreams out into the daylight. Learning more about what other people do is always a surefire way to get your own creativity flowing.

From this week on, actively pursue your dreams in small and large ways.

WEEK 7 SUMMARY

1. Do the dream and imagination exercises with your diary and try to articulate what your dream scenarios will be. Remember these throughout the week.

2. Choose an adventure and do it this week. The kids are welcome to come—that is up to you.

3. Create your GAL Dream file. Do it with your kids and they can create theirs as well.

4. Begin your MomsTown Dream Log.

5. Socialize your passion and actively attend social functions outside of the house to meet new people.

6. Consider throwing a party or attending a party. Get the plans started this week.

WEEK 8: BALANCE: HOW TO BEND WITHOUT BREAKING WHEN YOU'RE PULLED IN EVERY DIRECTION

We know you get pulled all over the place. This week we are going to work on balancing your relationships and the time put into them. Children, husbands, family, and friends are all vying for our attention, and we can do only so much. Learning how to set boundaries and put effort into your relationships will improve your quality of life and the relationships you have. By examining the nature of your relationships and how you contribute or make imbalanced contributions to them, you can take steps to balance your obligations and priorities. Ballet lessons, soccer practice, grocery shopping, fixing meals, trying to remember everything at once, and still having an alive, exciting relationship with your husband will wear you down to a nub unless you are proactively balancing your life in little everyday ways. Although your long list of duties as a mom can be frustrating at times, you need all of these relationships and they need you. Remembering the value of your relationships can help you balance the variety of demands. After all, moms are the pulse of the family and community. Working on our own personal juggling act with relationships can lend us strength.

Stay at Homework: Imagine that you are in the center of a room, and your husband, kids, in-laws, parents, friends, next-door neighbor, and kids' teachers are surrounding you. Now imagine all of these people pulling and stretching you to your limits. They grab your hands, legs, and clothes and pull in all directions as they make their requests of you. There are only so many directions, and there is only so far you can stretch while maintaining a sense of balance. In this chapter we are going to show you how to stretch without breaking—figuratively speaking, of course—and how to get more out of your relationships with everyone.

Quality vs. Quantity

In all relationships, there must be a balance between quality and quantity. Just because you are with your kids or husband, doesn't mean you are "putting in your time." Focusing on the people you are with is necessary for fulfillment and a healthy household. Here are some things to watch out for as you go through your day. Use this section to assess whether you are truly focusing on your relationships.

MAKING THE MOST OF YOUR TIME

Spending time with your kids means more than just sticking them in front of the TV. Be aware of what you are doing with them. Use the following to assess if you're spending quality time with your husband, friends, and family. Do you

• make a point to play interactive games with your kids?

• have a conversation with your kids after school, or allow them to walk straight in the door and over to the TV set?

- tune out when your children ask you question after question? Do you find yourself replying "I don't know" punctuated with a weary sigh?

- let your mind wander a million miles away as your husband tells you about his day?

- find yourself half present as your mom tells you about her vacation plans on the phone?

- feel too tired to even begin to tell a friend how your day is going?

- find yourself asking questions and not listening to the answers, then asking the same questions later?

- go to bed hoping your husband won't put any moves on you because you'd rather just go to sleep?

While we acknowledge that all moms do some of the above sometimes (after all, we're only human!), making these habits a way of life can be detrimental to the relationships most important to us. If you find yourself saying yes to some of the above, try to be more conscious of the effort you are making when you are with your children. Simply noticing when you are not really present with your children can help you modify some of these behaviors. Changing habits and patterns that persist when you're overtired and distracted can begin when you define your boundaries and learn to focus on enjoying the time you have with those you love. Getting the most out of your relationships can be fulfilling in so many ways. Not only do strengthened relationships support you more when you pursue your passions and dreams, but instead of draining you, they empower you.

Improving your relationships can bolster the work you do for yourself. It's a fact that you are a much stronger person when you are balanced and fulfilled in your relationships and support systems.

Stay at Homework: Allow yourself to focus on how much time—and the quality of the time—you spend with those closest to you. You will know when there is an imbalance. Make a list of at least six people in your life. This list should include kids, husband, friends, and family. Beside each person's name, express how balanced you think your relationship is. Write down your answers to the following questions:

Do you make time to focus on this person?
Do you pay attention and listen carefully to what this person says?
Do you make eye contact and show this person you care when you are around him or her?

Read over your responses. Everyone has areas they need to improve. Make a mental note as to what areas those are for you.

Relationship Factors

Imbalance in different aspects of your relationships can interfere with closeness and friendship. Some factors to watch include disrespect, lack of intimacy, lack of focus, and failure to set boundaries.

Respect

Let's start by assessing where you are in relation to respect.

Do you respect yourself?
Does your husband respect you?

Do your kids respect you?

Do your family and friends respect you?

Stay at Homework: If you are not getting respect, chances are you do not respect yourself. Take a moment to see yourself as others see you. Grab your diary and try to picture yourself in the eyes of those you love. Write an objective description of yourself—as objective as you can possibly be. Do you exude respect for your beliefs and needs? Do you stand up straight? Do you take care of your appearance? Respect begins with you and your respect for yourself and your relationships. Following the MomsTown program will help you find respect for yourself. After you find respect for yourself, the next step is finding it in your relationships.

Everyone needs to improve on their self-respect in some way. We'd like you to formulate a mantra that exudes respect for yourself and will remind you to act in ways that bring respect to you. Here are some mantras we have used:

I respect my beliefs, talents, sense of humor, and intellect.
I respect my creativity, interests, passions, and myself.
I respect who I am and what I stand for.

Stay at Homework: Grab your diary and come up with your own respect mantra. Remember to focus on your respect for yourself and those you love next time you visit your GAL Sanctuary.

Intimacy

Intimacy is another important component in any relationship. Let's assess where you stand when it comes to intimacy.

Do you allow yourself to listen to your own most intimate needs and thoughts? Can you admit it when you need a hug?

Do you initiate intimacy with your husband?

Do you hug your children daily? Do you make a point to ask about or listen to their innermost hopes and fears?

Do you hug your friends and family when you see them?

Do you say complimentary things regularly to your friends and family?

Do you find yourself avoiding intimacy with your husband?

Do you avoid intimate talks with your parents or extended family?

Becoming intimate with yourself and your own needs will help you forge intimacy with others.

Stay at Homework: Write a list in your GAL Diary of the most intimate things you have shared with your husband, kids, and family in the past three weeks. How do you express intimacy—physically or verbally? Are you afraid of intimacy?

Stay at Homework: This week try to deliberately express intimacy in your closest relationships. This can include physical or verbal intimacy. Here are some ideas:

Give a genuine hug when you see your friends, family, husband, and kids.

Give intimate compliments:

You look so nice in that color!

That haircut looks great on you.

You're so good at mowing the lawn.

It's good to see you.

Imbalance of the Giver/Taker

We all have potential to give and to take. Let's assess which you do more of. Answer the following questions.

Do you feel your husband takes more than he gives?

Do you find yourself unable to keep up with the requests your kids, husband, and family make of you?

Which relationships enrich your life?

Which relationships take from you?

Are your kids in the habit of helping and giving to the daily routine?

Do your friends give you support? Do they encourage you to succeed or to follow your passions? Do they create drama and need-based requests that take your energy?

In conversations with your family and friends, does the talking seem to be fifty-fifty?

Do you tend to listen more than talk, or do you dominate the conversation with your own talking?

The good news about the give/take balance is that it is up to you. You can change the way you engage with people accordingly. You are the only one you can control. Figuring out who in your life is a giver and who is a taker is the next step in gaining control of your relationships.

Stay at Homework: List your six closest relationships. You can add more if you like. List each person and loosely categorize him or her as a Giver, a Taker, or a person with whom you have a good balance. If a person currently gives or currently takes but you think he or she has the potential to balance, note that as well.

Do you have a girlfriend who constantly calls with an "emergency" and needs you to drop everything to hear her side of the story? When you call for her support, is she too busy with her life to give you the time of day? If you have this kind of relationship in your life, distance yourself from it. Moms are too busy to tolerate unbalanced friendships; we need friends who give back as much as they take. One of our moms, Taneisha, says, "Once I looked at who was always taking my time but not really giving me much back, I realized I had a couple of friends I didn't want in my life anymore. It was simply a matter of looking at patterns of behavior I had fallen into with these women. They would call and I would drop everything in order to help them, until their next drama. I might be in the middle of a hectic schedule, but no matter what, their crisis was always deemed more important. When I would have problems and need support, they would scarcely acknowledge it. I was able to see this clearly when I looked at everyone in terms of Givers and Takers. In these terms, I also found a way to balance my relationship with my husband. After evaluating it, I realized I had put myself in a position where I never really told him what I wanted but always asked what he wanted. I have since begun telling him what I'd like to give and what I would like him to give and we've established a much more balanced relationship."

As you become more in tune with the support you give and receive, try to pinpoint those relationships that are balanced in your life as opposed to those that are not. You will achieve your goals more easily when interacting with people who add to the quality of your life.

Boundaries

Boundaries are tools to help you keep your relationships in check, your energy intact, and your priorities in line. Let's assess whether or not you set good boundaries. Do you

have a hard time saying no?

think you have to put your best effort forward for every request, from your kids to your mother-in-law?

think you should always be at the beck and call of your child's teacher for chaperone duties and volunteer events?

try to make everyone happy, disregarding your goals in the process?

avoid revealing your thoughts and feelings because it might cause discontent or go against the grain?

care more what people think of your efforts to meet their needs than about what *your* needs are?

often have fears and feelings of obligation that come from the fear that you will appear to be a terrible mother in others' eyes?

If these questions speak to you, you may need to work on setting boundaries. This is one of the biggest steps in improving your relationships. When boundaries are clearly defined, much of the stress is taken off you. You begin to know and understand your limits, and so does the other person in the relationship.

Chances are if you're trying to take care of your family, your friends, your mom and dad, and your pets, you've had a little trouble sticking to boundaries. We have found, as you might imagine, that it's not uncommon for women, and moms in particular, to have difficulty identifying their limits. Moms, especially SAHMs, are notorious for trying to do everything for everyone. We think we can do it all, and some of us (let's admit it) feel guilty for staying at home. So we think everything in the home and beyond is our responsibility. We begin to convince ourselves that every task under the sun qualifies as in bounds: our kid's dentist appointment, the homemade chocolate cake for our friend's birthday party, our mother's requests that we organize the family Thanksgiving, Halloween decorations for the yard, the bake sale, and anything else that comes up. Not having boundaries is a recipe for disaster of the worst kind. If you don't set limits, you will automatically experience an increase in guilt, resentment, and fatigue, and ultimately not give your loved ones, or yourself, the time deserved.

Here are some things to remember when you are considering setting your boundaries.

- No one likes a martyr, and that's what you become when you sacrifice yourself for others.

- You are doing your loved ones a disservice when you do not clearly define boundaries.

- People like to know what is expected of them so they can be sure they are being the best friend, mother-in-law, babysitter they can be.

- By setting boundaries you are respecting your limits and your needs.

- Setting boundaries builds self-esteem, and doing a regular assessment of what you can handle is a responsible thing to do for everyone involved.

- You are more likely to succeed if you set boundaries than if you try to do everything for everyone.

- No one respects someone who needs people to need them. By setting boundaries, you are acknowledging that people can rely on you to an extent, but not in an unlimited, dysfunctional way.

- Your identity is not defined by others' dependence on you.

- Disappointing others is necessary in your quest to find yourself.

One of our MomsTown members, Tricia, recalls a very useful boundary she was able to set up. "My mother-in-law graciously offered to take my twins one afternoon a week. Before this arrangement, we used to play the guessing game about when was a good time for my mother-in-law to babysit the babies. It was awful. Sometimes I felt I was imposing on her and other times I felt she was doing the same to me. Finally we came up with a particular time and day of the week. Every Tuesday afternoon she takes the babies. That way, both of us know we aren't bothering each other. She knows that's her time with the babies and she won't be bugging me or showing up at a bad time, and I know I can count on her help that time every week instead of asking her to babysit when it may not really suit her, and the babies know that is their special time with Grandmama." By setting a boundary, which in this case was a certain day every week, Tricia didn't have to go over her schedule every week with her mother-in-law, and neither had to feel they were working around the other's schedule.

Setting boundaries can take many forms: scheduling, saying no, sticking to your guns when you feel something doesn't apply to your authentic self, or distancing yourself from certain friends who have a draining effect on you. While it may be hard to get used to saying no, in the long run you will all benefit.

You Don't Have the Watercooler Anymore: The Ethel Principle

Earlier in the book, we talked about finding your "Ethel." We'd like to expand on that idea. MomsTown believes your girlfriends are important. Having a good girlfriend can keep you balanced in other relationships in your life. As we've pointed out, Lucy needed Ethel; every woman needs an Ethel. We cannot overstate how important your friends are—that is, your *real* friends. Those are the friends who support you in your endeavors, who immediately see your talents and vision for what they are, and who immediately make you feel like yourself. They are your cheering section when you doubt yourself, and the ones who say, "I knew you could do it." It is important to surround yourself with women who support and love you.

SAHMs have the unique pressure of being away from the typical co-worker community that has replaced the sewing bee of yore. Many SAHMs have left a vibrant built-in social life around the corporate watercooler only to find themselves suddenly out of the loop. Even if you didn't leave behind a happening watercooler scene at your office, that doesn't mean that you feel completely comfortable being isolated at home with the kids. No one told you how to prepare for becoming a stay-at-home mother. Unlike at an office job, you don't have a social system built into your daily life. After leaving the maternity ward with your new baby, you may feel you've been dropped off on a desert island to fend for yourself. Even if it's been a few years, you may not have regained that sense of social connectedness you had before you had your children.

It is crucial to your sanity to feel that you have a social life to call your own if you want one. This can make every other responsibility you have bearable. Giving yourself an outlet with your peers does wonders for your perspective. Your SAHM girlfriends understand what you go through on a daily basis as a mother. They can understand the demanding challenges of taking care of children, pursuing your own life dreams, and the issues that can arise in a marriage. Most important, if they are good friends, they are on your side! They are your cheering section, your pal to have a glass of wine with or someone to call when you need a shoulder to lean on. Know that your friends can be your oasis. They will be your lifeline as you attempt to get a life. Value them, invest energy in them, and enjoy them!

Girlfriends are your medicine, and putting time aside for your own social outings can be good for you. One of our moms, Becca, finds she must set aside time with her friends and family, outside her kids and husband. "Every so often, I go off by myself for a couple of days and visit my friends . . . without the husband or children. It makes me a much better mother, believe me. My husband is completely amenable to this arrangement. He goes camping with his friends for a week every November, so he feels it's only fair that I get a break every now and then."

Stay at Homework: In this next week, think about who your real friends are. If you have not found friends that you can relate to, make an effort to meet some. Even if you have a solid group of friends, it is still necessary to bring new people into your life on a regular basis. Is there someone in your neighborhood or community or a mother of one of your children's friends who you have always meant to get in touch with and get to know better but haven't taken the time? This week, make an effort to introduce yourself to a new person. Make time. Friends don't just happen; like anything rewarding, they take work.

YOUR KIDS WILL THANK YOU

At MomsTown, as we've said before, if you put active energy toward your own happiness, your kids will thank you in the long run. Remember, this book is not about your kids, it's about you. How can you get more out of your relationship with your kids? By getting a life! Your kids will thank you if you put time and energy into your own life and goals. They will learn to do the same for themselves. That said, there are a few tips we've compiled about getting more out of our relationships with our kids.

Avoid yes/no questions. Ask open-ended questions. To upgrade the quality of time with your kids, ask questions that can't be answered with a simple yes or no. These questions require thought, consideration, and more than a few words. If you start early, once they reach the teenage years, they will be in the habit of telling you about their activities in school. Rather than asking, "Did you have a good day in school?" ask "What did you like about school today?" and "Why?"

Focus on them when you talk with them. When your kids do answer your questions or ask you questions, try to make eye contact and focus. We know this isn't always possible, but when you can, it matters. Making them feel important and making yourself focus on them increases their self-esteem and yours. Are your children interrupting you on the phone a lot? If so, they may be trying to tell you they need more attention.

Be a role model. Be aware of the kind of example you set for your kids. Do you spend the whole day doing for others and never for yourself? If so, chances are they won't have all that much respect for you and may fall into the same pattern as they get older. Do you take care of your appearance and deal responsibly with your obligations and schedule? If not, they may develop these same bad habits. Everything you do for yourself sets a conscious or unconscious example for your kids. One of our moms, Martha, said, "I used the word *stupid* one day when I was talking about someone who cut me off in traffic. That night, my three-year-old called his little sister stupid and I couldn't believe it, since I had never let him use language like that. I remembered where he heard it after I questioned him and he told me that *I* had said it! I really watch my language now. They really pick up so many things you wouldn't even consider!"

Don't talk critically about "friends of the family" in front of your kids. Sooner or later that might get back to those supposed friends, and it sets a bad example for your kids to do the same. Practice what you preach. You are the number one role model for your kids; act like it. If you become a terrific Gal with a terrific life, it will only have positive effects on them.

Talk to others about your children's good behavior in front of them. If you want your kids to be athletic, you be athletic. If you want your children to read books, then you read books. Practice and explain random acts of kindness to your children. Achieve your personal goals and your children will be more likely to achieve theirs.

The SAHM Privilege

Redefine the role of a SAHM not only for yourself but for your children. It is a privilege, not a luxury, as many may think, to stay home. It's also not a given, as your children may think. If you elevate your idea of your role in their lives as a SAHM to the status of privilege, your kids will see it that way, too. Be aware of how you portray your choice to stay at home and raise them. Pride, privilege, and choice should be in the definition of a SAHM.

Discuss this regularly with your kids and be sure they understand why you choose to stay at home and how lucky you all are that you can do that.

Stay at Homework: Take some time to bring the SAHM privilege up to your kids in conversation this week. Avoid preaching to them about how lucky they might be and concentrate on illuminating how happy you are that you have this opportunity to be at home with them.

There are so many triumphs and successes that come in different packages as a SAHM. Even if you're running a business out of your home like our mom Betsy, you get the rewards of being there for your children and making a home for them. She says of her greatest triumphs, "They come in quiet little moments which take me by surprise. For example, today my oldest daughter [four] really made me smile. She is very much into the princess scene, and while taking a cute quiz at Disney.com on 'Which Princess are you most like?' there was a question that really stood out. When asked where she would choose to live, there were options such as a castle, a palace, a grand manor, or a cottage, but she chose 'in my family's home.' Wow. She'd rather live right here—even though I won't paint the house pink—than move to a palace. That is a little triumph for me."

BE A MOMSTOWN QUARTERBACK: CALL THE SHOTS AND COMMUNICATE THE GAME PLAN

Not a lot of people would think of a mom as a quarterback, but as you already know we look at things differently here in MomsTown. We define a quarterback as an on-field general, the one who calls the shots. The quarterback controls the plays and is ultimately responsible for the team. As a mom, you call the shots in the home; you strategize about getting your family to the end zone or winning the goals you've set. As a SAHM, you make a lot of decisions that determine the direction of your family, or "team." The daily schedule can be seen as a game plan. It's your job to create the game plan, stick to it, and communicate the details of it to the rest of your family.

At MomsTown we believe in sticking to your own schedule as well as sticking to one with your kids. This message applies specifically to younger kids. Kids need a secure, regular schedule and confidence. A schedule wards off any sense of insecurity and nervousness. If they know what to expect, your kids will operate in the offensive mode. When they don't know what to expect, they will operate in the defensive mode. Sticking to the schedule you set for yourself, like the Hot Iron, regular workouts, and regimented planning will benefit not only you but also your kids. As the family quarterback, you must let your family know what the game plan is ahead of time. As a mom, you keep your schedule faithfully and prepare your family for that daily schedule.

Don't put your children in the position of being panicked by not giving them a solid routine to rely on. If you provide a secure, pre-dictable routine for your kids, you're giving them the building blocks of self-assurance and confidence.

Here are some ways to help your children adjust to the schedule of the day or any changes it might have:

⬩ Go over the next day's schedule with your kids the night before so they know what to expect. This, of course, is more necessary with younger kids who are with you throughout the day.

⬩ Dwell on some fun things that might be involved or different by preparing them the night before; for example:

"When Mommy goes to the gym you'll get to play in the gym nursery with the other kids" or "you'll get to go to Auntie's or Grandma's."

"Tomorrow is art day and we'll get to draw and paint."

"Tomorrow we are going on an adventure to the zoo!"

Not only will your kids feel secure because they understand the plan but they will put up less resistance because they will be looking forward to it. You'll have an easier time carrying out your plans with them on your side.

Family and the Holiday Thing

Holidays can be stressful. But we also think holidays provide a way for you to create your own memories and traditions, not just follow in the footsteps of others. They can help you strengthen your relationships with your other family members, too. By forging ahead with your own ideas and dreams of the holidays, rather than conforming to everyone else's expectations of them, you are creating your own life and creating a unique tradition for your family.

The MomsTown philosophy gives you permission to modify family customs and make your own unique traditions. Don't feel bound to your mother's way of doing Thanksgiving or Christmas. There are ways to make it your own while still including your family. Making your holidays the way you want them may mean

- not allowing yourself to feel worn out or stressed.

- setting boundaries far in advance about what you will and won't do.

- keeping plans simple. Avoid complicated, drawn-out obligations.

- planning months in advance, not waiting until the week before. (This includes who and what you will have at the meal. Delegate! Assign everyone a dish if you're hosting.)

- taking a trip rather than staying at home for the traditional celebration.

- remembering this is your holiday as much as anyone else's, and you deserve to enjoy it, too.

- buying presents all year long when you see them or they are on sale, rather than doing all of your Christmas shopping at the last minute along with the masses.

- letting all of your extended family know as soon as you've made your holiday plans and then sticking with them. One of our moms, Lucy, found that when she does this, "Everyone knows up front what we will be doing and where, and there won't be any last-minute confusion or hurt feelings."

Stay at Homework: Look on your calendar and see what you can do to make the upcoming holiday season easier. Figure out what you can do to make the holidays more fun for yourself.

One of our moms, Mindy, reassessed some details of her holiday routine. "I no longer stress over getting the perfect photo of the kids and Christmas cards mailed to over a hundred people. I send Christmas cards to about thirty and the remainder get either a Valentine's card or an Easter/Spring greeting. Christmas is so busy, this allows me to spread out some of the time-consuming things I enjoy doing. I bake less now than I used to, and try to just enjoy letting the kids make a mess."

Throughout this week and going forward, we ask you to examine your relationships and what they give and take from you. As we've said before, relationships are a core part of your strength. They can build you up or break you down. You decide which, by observing your current patterns and establishing new, healthy, empowering patterns.

A GAL'S HUBBY

The MomsTown program recognizes that husbands are a fundamental part of our lives, and balancing our relationship with them is a way to help us get it all! This week we'd like to go over some of the MomsTown rules for relationships with husbands.

RULE # 1: GET OVER IT

The first thing we'd like to say is, Get over it. Your husband will never see things completely the way you do. That's the way it is, and you can go ahead and regard it as a fact of life. There are compromises to be made, treaties to be forged, but there will never be the exact same perspective, especially if one of you—*you*—is staying home and taking care of the kids and the other—*he*—is not. There are inherent differences that will require understanding and acceptance by both you and your husband. Yes, men are from Mars. This is scary but true. But you still married this guy, you love him, and you want to maintain a relationship with him. There are ways to bridge even the most seemingly impossible gaps.

Margaret has decided to get over it after five years of marriage. "I remember getting advice from friends of mine who had been married longer. When I was in the first couple of years of marriage, I used to get so angry when my husband didn't understand my perspective on anything, from how to clean the house to what to fix the kids for dinner to when I would go out. My friends said, 'That's just the way it is, he's not going to change, we know how it is, we all married the same man.' Looking back, I realize I was expecting my husband and me to have the same outlook on everything when that was actually an impossible expectation. I also realized I had two choices: I could continue to nag about the socks on the floor, or I could move on and work on other parts of our relationship. I did the latter and other parts of our relationship blossomed. Now I find myself grateful that we have the same perspective on values, disciplining our kids, and loving and supporting each other to the best of our ability. I understand that I accept and even love our differences, and I concentrate on being in agreement about the things that matter. Men are different creatures, it's just the way it is. (But that doesn't mean I can't hope he'll pick up his socks.)" Find a common ground with your husband. You may have differences, but we're willing to bet you can find things to come together on as well. Focus on the positives, not the negatives in your relationship.

RULE # 2: HE'S NOT YOUR GIRLFRIEND

Your husband is not your girlfriend, but as we will explain later, you need to be his. He's not a woman, your "Ethel," or a chick. In fact, he's the furthest thing from this. And that is okay. He doesn't need to be your girlfriend, he is your partner and your lover. He won't get some things about you, but as long as he's putting forth a solid, loving effort to understand, he gets points. He needs to be there to support you, love you, rub your shoulders, and help you raise your children, but it's okay if he doesn't understand why the Kodak commercial made you burst into tears.

One of our MomsTown moms, Marissa, told us, "I tell my girlfriends about some things, and I tell my husband others. It's not that I want to keep certain things from my husband, but some issues—like outfits, funny stories, emotional girl subjects, or shopping advice—get a better response from my girlfriends than from my husband. I share my hopes, dreams, and stories about the kids with my husband. Every relationship brings out different things in me. I don't expect my husband to 'get' everything my girlfriends and I talk about—or vice versa."

RULE # 3: BUT YOU CAN BE HIS GIRLFRIEND

As for you, you can benefit from being his girlfriend—that is, the woman you were before you had kids. We know this is not entirely possible and we're talking degrees here, not absolutes. You can still be the woman he married who loved to sneak into a dark corner and brush against him, who would wear a new, tight dress just to surprise him, or who left little love notes in his briefcase. The girlfriend explores other parts of her relationship with her man, outside of what to eat for dinner, what the kids did in school today, or the number of diapers she changed. It's healthy for him, and most important, it's healthy for you.

After having children, you find you are in love with each other in other ways. A deep bond is set with the birth and raising of your kids. However important and necessary and deep that bond is, it doesn't have to be the only bond. Rekindle your girlfriend within. Allow yourself to have great sex with him, look deep into his eyes and wonder what he'll do next. We will expand more on this later in this chapter.

RULE # 4: DATE NIGHT IS NOT A LUXURY, IT'S A NECESSITY

MomsTown has very strong opinions about date night. You *must* have it. We don't care what you have to do to arrange it, just make sure it happens. Maybe it means bribing a babysitter, digging coins from behind the cushions in the couch to pay her, or begging a family member to take care of the kids. But however you swing it, you need it, and your relationship needs it. One of the first things Heather's pediatrician told her and her husband after the birth of their first baby was to make sure they had a date night once a week, if only for an hour. If you don't have a stable relationship with your husband, and the time to develop and respect that relationship, your family will feel the vibrations, however minor you think they may be.

Telling the kids that mommy and daddy need time together or asking them not to interrupt your conversations sets a precedent and shows your children your relationship deserves respect. If they know mommy and daddy are happy, they will be happy. It is a law of the family. The time you give your relationship adds to the likelihood it will be stable and good. This gives your whole family peace, happiness, and a sense of stability.

Stay at Homework: Arrange a date night for this week with your husband.

RULE # 5: VENUS IN THE HOME, MARS IN THE OFFICE

Recognize and accept the differences between you and your husband in your daily routines and realms. You spend your days in an entirely different realm from your husband's. Yours is the home, with the kids and a million other things to divide your attention among. Even if you work from home, your surroundings are different from your husband's office, warehouse, hospital, or other public environment. His world consists of co-workers, clients, projects, child-free bathroom breaks, and meals out. It's easy to find yourself frustrated when your husband asks you what you did today. Often moms assume there is a subtext (Did you accomplish anything *big* while I was slaving away to support the family?). You may ask how his day was and think, "Did you enjoy a lunch with your friendly co-workers as I raced around after the kids and ate my lunch standing up?" This is a common situation. It is hard to see things from the other person's perspective after a long day and when both of you are exhausted.

With SAHM schedules and chores it is hard to have the same, re-solved feelings of accomplishment your husband gains from his work-ing environment. Often completing your daily list doesn't carry the same official sense of success that the completion of your husband's big project at work might. But there *are* some ways to keep yourself in check when you begin feeling frustrated with the division of responsibility.

Acknowledge that you both have stress, albeit different kinds of stress, and that both kinds are real. Often having a family puts a whole new group of pressures on a husband's work, achievements, and stress level. Being the only breadwinner can be difficult.

Communicate about the pressures you both feel without blaming or finger pointing. Talk to him about the pressures he feels rather than fo-cusing on his lack of comprehension about what you do on a daily basis. This type of communication can illuminate a variety of issues, and make them less scary and less likely to get to the boiling-over point.

Ask him about his day and really listen to his response. He will ap-preciate the voluntary attention and will most likely follow your exam-ple. Sympathize with his stress of the workday and emphasize that you need him to do the same for you. A significant difference in work envi-ronments inevitably brings frustrations, but if you both acknowledge this, it is easy to overcome. Simply being aware of the different challenges each of you faces and communicating about them in a regular way can make a huge difference. Venting frustrations, resentment, and guilt through communication and conversation rather than hostile confrontation can deflect potential arguments. One of our MomsTown members, Gabby, relates how much this change of perspective has strengthened her relationship with her husband: "When Tim and I talk about what happened at work that day, I feel connected to his office world. Oftentimes when he tells me about challenges or problems at work, I have ideas or suggestions for him from a fresh and objective perspective that he appreciates. These engaged conversations cut back on the polarity of 'his' world versus 'my' world and make me feel as if I am a part of his office life as well as his home life and that he includes me as part of his *entire* day."

Even if you have different demands during the day, you can do things together that unite your familial and life goals. Communicate openly about what you expect out of your life, your family, and your values. Often when we are with someone for a while, we do not actively check in on these issues. It is always a good idea to keep talking about values, beliefs, and expectations.

Dream together. Share your dreams with your husband. Make him aware of the big picture as you see it. Check in and see what his dreams are. How do your dreams mesh? Each of you should support the other in your respective dreams. If he wants a promotion to senior vice president of his company, or ultimately to have his own company, know that and check in regularly to see how his goals are progressing. If you want to start your own Web-based business or yoga studio out of the home, share this dream with him. Share and commiserate, but keep the home team together, as a unit. Even if you seem to be on separate missions throughout the day, remember you are both working hard toward the same goals in the long run.

Plan a dream vacation to take in a year, or five years. Find your common goals and move toward them—together. When you get there, you'll have each other to thank. The important part is for each of you to communicate and to see things through the other's eyes. One of our MomsTown members, Lucille, says, "Vacations are a fun topic of conversation when it seems you can't think of anything to talk about with each other besides the kids." Talking about vacations is fun and creates something for the two of you to work toward.

Stay at Homework: Try to begin researching and talking about your dreams with your husband. Work toward planning your dream vacation with him. Take beginning steps this week. After the kids have gone to bed, open a bottle of wine and have a brainstorming session on destinations for your dream vacation.

A Gal's Guide to Getting It On: Sex for the New Gal

Oh, where to start! Sex is important in so many, many ways: your health, your husband's health, your spiritual and physical relationship, your complexion, confidence, attitude, and let's not forget, your recreational enjoyment! If you roll your eyes when your husband tries to put the not-so-smooth moves on you, think only about your kids being in the next room when he suggests having sex, or feign a headache, tummy ache, "that time of the month," or fatigue when the truth is that you really aren't into it, this is the part for you.

We understand what it's like to have children and to have been married for a while. The chemistry isn't as apparent as it used to be, and the stress of a long, busy day can be overwhelming. Your boobs and bottom just don't look or feel like they used to. How do you make yourself feel sexy after all you went through today? This is an entirely normal feeling, but it's not inevitable. You *can* be sexy. We are going to show you how to turn off the mom and turn on the Gal.

We have some tips to keep things in the bedroom fun for both of you. Sex can be a great way to reconnect with your husband outside of the kids and household responsibilities. It can be a healthy, natural way for you to feel young and spunky. Like everything else, though, you've got to put yourself in the right frame of mind. You can't feel like you are forcing yourself to have sex. Wanting to have sex regularly is a lifestyle, not something you have to fit in your schedule or treat like a punch-in time card.

◆ GAL Intimacy Tips ◆

Building a foundation of intimacy is one way to lay the groundwork for a good sex life. Intimacy is a delicate balance of gestures and considerations that build throughout the days, weeks, and months, not just ten minutes before sex. We believe that if you follow through on some of these tips, he will do the same for you. You can't expect someone to give to you when you don't give to them. Of course, everything should be done in moderation. Use common sense. If you feel you are always giving 100 percent and getting back less than that from him, rethink your approach. Otherwise, don't be shy about what you can bring to this relationship. By taking care of your husband, you are taking care of yourself. Here are some simple ways to make your relationship more intimate.

• Touch your husband in intimate, everyday ways. A hand on his shoulder as you pass by him in the hall, however small, builds intimacy between you.

- Make an effort to offer a foot rub or shoulder rub—the more you do for him, the more he will do for you. Establish small yet deliberate ways of being intimate throughout the day, and in the evening when it's time to have sex, being together will feel more natural. This will help you get in the mood when the time comes. Remember, it's not just for your husband, it's for you!

- Compliment him. We forget to do this regularly. We become fixed in our ways of interacting and forget that we all need compliments. Tell him a color looks handsome on him or that you've always liked his eyes. Remember why you fell in love with him and remind him of this. When you compliment him, he will compliment you back.

- Surprise him. Surprise him with his favorite meal, snack, or movie. Do little things that remind him you are thinking about him all day. Put together a picnic lunch for your date and don't tell him where you're taking him. Show him how you want to be surprised and romanced. Showing by action instead of words is much easier and rewarding. This can be so much fun that you'll be patting yourself on the back when you see how much he appreciates it.

- Do little things for your husband. Bring him a cup of coffee in the morning. You know what small special kind acts you can do that he will appreciate. Does he want more of your time, does he love little gifts, does he want to talk about work more? This doesn't mean you're doing everything for him, you are just recognizing his particular needs and he will notice. In small, significant ways, we can make him feel special. Make a point to show him you are aware of his preferences. By making your husband feel special, you are letting him know that you love him and strengthening a relationship that will ultimately support you more and give you more balance in your life. By having a devoted, loving husband in a fulfilling, intimate relationship, you are that much closer to getting it all!

Gradually putting these tips in motion is a good way to achieve more intimacy. You will find with minor yet simple actions on a daily basis, you can establish more trust and intimacy in all areas of your relationship with your husband.

Think Like a Girlfriend—Not a Wife—in the Bed

We've said this before and we'll say it again. It's very easy to change your approach to a relationship. You may have been together for ten years. Try to think like you did before marriage and kids. We know it's a challenge, but it is rewarding to change your perspective and help change his.

Stay at Homework: Think back for a moment. Grab your diary and answer some of the questions that follow. What were some of the most exciting things you did before marriage?

Where was the most exciting place you had sex?

What was the most outlandish position you tried?

How did you feel getting ready for a first date with a guy you had a crush on?

What outfit made you feel like the most attractive woman in the room?

Where did you go when you went out with your girlfriends?

How did you act when you found you were in love with your husband?

Did you do anything in particular to seduce your husband? If so, what?

When sex wasn't available to you each night, did you want it
more?

What efforts did you make with hair, makeup, clothes, etc., to
make yourself attractive?

Stay at Homework: Pick one of the above memories and reenact it this
week.

Stay at Homework: Next time you get ready to go on your date with
your husband (and you should be having these regularly by now), put
yourself together the way you would have when you were trying to be
noticed. Dressing and thinking like you were when you were single is
fun and helps you break out of some of your typical routines.

Thinking like a girlfriend helps you distance yourself from your
responsibilities as a mother. Thoughts of your kids quickly disrupt any
sexy vibes you might be cooking up. Try to stay focused on you, not
your kids. We give you permission to be playful, enjoy sex, and make it
a priority! To rekindle your libido, you have to rekindle your thoughts
and attitude.

◆ GAL Sex Tips ◆

Finding your sex drive after it's been stomped on by a thousand
tiny feet can be tough. It will take an adventurous spirit and some risks.
We have heard from so many moms that they do want to have sex, but
have difficulty getting into the mood. It is different for every woman, so
do some serious, no-holds-barred research and find out what works for
you. Figuring out the ways in which you feel most comfortable having
sex is like finding your passion. Even if you have had a hysterectomy or
early menopause, that doesn't mean you still can't have fun. You may
have to search, but in the end you will be rewarded.

Here are some ways to explore your hidden sexual diva.

• Pay attention to your cycle. What time of the month is the best time to have sex? You actually have hormones on your side a week or so after your cycle. This varies with all women, so figure out what time that is for you. Use your hormones, plan for a date, and make the moves. You'll find your body eager to cooperate.

• Forget about the kids for once. If you typically find thoughts of your kids interfering when you're intimate with your husband, make a point this week to have a babysitter, friend, or family member take the kids to a movie while you and your husband are home. If you can afford it, rent a hotel room and go there after your date. It's easier to get the kids out of your mind when they are not in the next room. If you decide to stay home and the kids are just in bed down the hall, try to focus. Focus on you and your man.

• Figure out what your fantasy is. Do you have one? Think hard. If not, think through a few scenarios and see what works for you.

Stay at Homework: Grab your diary and write down a fantasy. If you don't have one already, make one up.

• Ask your husband what his fantasy is. Chances are, just by asking, you'll open a new level of conversation that makes you feel more intimate with him. You don't have to reenact it exactly, especially if it makes you uncomfortable, but it will give you a lot more insight to what his turn-ons are and little touches you can add to spice things up. You don't need to ask him in the bedroom, unless you feel comfortable doing that. It may add too much pressure. Try to do it in a conversational way while at dinner alone or in the car. Don't let yourself be overly serious about it. Relax, smile, and laugh as you talk. It can be a fun topic, rather than embarrassing.

• Romantic movies can be fun. Some of these movies help put you in the mood. Date-night movies can be a fun way to spend a romantic night together. Make them as sexy as you are comfortable with.

• Lingerie can be a sexy way to dress yourself up for the bedroom. It can be as daring as you're comfortable with. If it suits you, T-shirt and boxers are fine. Figure out what's right for you and your husband. Having lingerie or an outfit you have purchased especially for the bedroom can make you feel sexy. And if you feel sexy, you feel empowered.

• Wear your birthday suit. Being naked is just as much fun as lingerie. If you don't have the budget to get nice lingerie, we can promise your husband will be pleasantly surprised when you slip into bed naked instead of wearing that old flannel nightgown. Try it this week and see how it goes.

• Find an erotic place to have sex. Sex doesn't always have to be in the bedroom. Maybe you could meet him at the office after everyone has gone home, or in the woods on a hike on one of your dates. Be creative and do what sounds exciting to you.

Seduction Takes Time

One of the reasons you might not be feeling like the sexy Gal you are is that you're trying to have sex during the only ten minutes you spend with your husband alone before you fall asleep. By adding little touches throughout your daily routine and interactions with your husband, you can build a more intimate relationship. Many of the tips we are going to give you are simple and perhaps obvious. Regardless of how small or large these gestures are, they are important. We encourage you to notice the details, intimacy, and little romantic surprises that can bring your relationship alive by integrating them into your daily lives.

As we said before, think like a girlfriend. The flirting, touching, alluding to, and fantasizing about sex can be done all day, even a week beforehand. There are several ways to set yourself and your husband up for romance at the end of the night that will leave you breathless for sex instead of dreading it. You must massage your own libido and his in small, simple, consistent ways.

Take a deep breath, relax your shoulders, and go into this with a smile. Remember, this can be fun. There are plenty of ways to make excitement and anticipation build during the day for both of you as you wait to see each other in the evening. Below are some tips on how to get started.

Absence makes the heart grow fonder. Make a point to think about your husband when you are away from him. Take a few minutes when you are in the grocery store or waiting for your kids in the car after school or practice, or while they are napping, to imagine things you might have done before you were married. Imagine a passionate kiss, a feature of his you love, and being intimate with him. Imagine being with your husband that evening as your fantasy. This is a tangible, real fantasy that you can fulfill by seeing him and being with him in the evening. If you focus on what you love about him during the day, you will treasure it more when you see him at night.

Leave small messages and surprises. It only takes a moment to write a short note on a Post-it and leave it in his briefcase. Writing an e-mail or leaving a voice mail for him while he is at work can remind him that you are thinking about him and build his expectations to see you in the evening. The note can be as simple as "I can't wait to see you tonight," "I am thinking of you," or "I have a surprise for you when you get home." It can do wonders for his mood.

Flirt. Just because the kids are in the room, that doesn't mean you can't flirt. Small comments, intimate touches, eye contact, and smiles qualify as flirting. All of these small gestures add to the relationship you have with your husband outside the realm of family and kids.

Plan a surprise date. Take turns planning your regular dates away from the kids. Make it a surprise so that each time one of you is not involved in planning. Make it romantic, down to the details. Don't forget sexy underwear for afterward!

Wear something he has never seen before. This could be a new dress, heels, hairstyle, skirt, sexy top, or even a new perfume. One of the things that keeps us feeling we are in a boring routine is our familiarity. Making yourself unfamiliar in any way can be exciting for both of you. You will feel sexier and he will agree. Even if he doesn't notice right away, it will still be more fun to wear something out of the ordinary.

Pay attention to atmosphere. It is not silly to put on romantic music or turn the lights down low. In fact, changing the atmosphere is a deliberate way of signaling that you are interested in being intimate. Put on some music that makes you feel sexy. Is there a song or record you used to listen to when you first started dating? If so, that's the perfect way to set the tone.

Create code words and code phrases. Make a secret language for you and your husband. This can be something fun you come up with together. Choose a word that can be a code for sex and use it when you talk with him on the phone while he's at work. Secrets are sexy and sharing them can be great foreplay.

Stay at Homework: Grab your diary and think of your own little creative way to spice up your relationship and build romantic expectations with your husband. Then put it into practice this week!

"Sexy" and "Mom" Are Not Mutually Exclusive

The MomsTown program encourages you to make your life a marriage of your best qualities. You can be a mom and sexy at the same time. Your confidence, attitude, and improving physique from your regular workouts should already be fueling your inherently attractive qualities. You can have terrific sex with your husband and still be a goddess mother who knows how to make macaroni necklaces, do all of the grocery shopping, and tuck in her kids at night. It is possible to have it all.

Stay at Homework: Grab your diary and write down what your attractive qualities were before you were married. Which of these qualities can you pay more attention to or remind yourself of in daily ways?

The word *mom,* and its cultural identity, isn't something we normally associate with *sexy*. Why not? MomsTown has proved to countless moms they can be both. Your husband wants to have a romantic relationship and sex life, too, whether that is obvious right now or not. It can be easy to tap into both of your needs for intimacy and sex if you emphasize communication, fun, excitement, and mutual consideration in detailed, easy ways every day.

It is essential to realize that everything you dream about can be created from what you have now. The grass may always seem greener on the other side. Put some time into making the grass green on *your* side. Take the elements you've remembered from when you were a girlfriend and combine them with your life now. You *can* have it all!

WEEK 8 SUMMARY

1. If you get frustrated, go back to Week 1 and read the GAL Truths.

2. Play an interactive game with your children the next time they go for the TV.

3. Work on listening carefully when you ask a question.

4. Develop a respect mantra and say it the next time you find yourself doing something that is not conducive to self-respect.

5. Make a point to be intimate this week with three people. Pay them compliments or give them a hug when you see them.

6. Begin noticing your present relationships. As you interact in each one, note to yourself whether you are a Giver or a Taker.

7. Plan a date night with your husband and make it happen.

8. Give some special attention to livening up your sex life and planning a sexy surprise. Choose one surprise you can plan for your husband this week.

9. Look ahead to the next family holiday. Figure out how you can work toward making it less stressful.

WEEK 9: THE VIRTUE OF VANITY: WHY GRANDMA WEARS LIPSTICK

MomsTown believes you're never too old to feel young and take good care of your appearance and your body. Heather's grandmother, Nellie, never leaves her house without a great shade of pink lipstick and a pair of earrings that match her outfit. She does it because she knows it shows herself and everyone else that she cares about her appearance. Her vanity is a virtue and she doesn't forget it, no matter what her age does to her physical appearance—her inner self is composed and well nurtured.

Despite all of the attention we're giving the inner Gal, the MomsTown program does not ignore the outer Gal by any stretch. We believe wholeheartedly in making sure we look good. At MomsTown, vanity is an essential element when it comes to getting it all! This week we will focus on some tips that will help better reflect that inner gorgeous Gal in your look and image and will keep you feeling young and adventurous.

We will share tips you can incorporate into your daily routine that complement your diligent physical work (your workouts) and your emotional work (exploring your inner Gal). By taking care of your exterior—from makeup to hygiene—you are maintaining more than your looks. Just as with regular workouts, the act of taking care of yourself creates a positive attitude, self-esteem, and confidence. Creating routines that nurture your looks and your outward persona builds confidence within. We promise that if you follow our tips and discover and develop your own vanity skills, you will feel much better about yourself. And you'll understand why Grandma wears lipstick!

MomsTown regards vanity as a virtue because it tells the world you care about and value yourself. In MomsTown, we do not define vanity as a narcissistic quality involving hours of primping in the morning, looking down your nose at others' looks, or believing you are more gorgeous than the other moms on your block. We take a more positive approach toward vanity. This approach leads to a powerful, well-nurtured physical self, which serves to balance and reaffirm your emotional self. If you're feeling frumpy on the outside, your mood will match. If you look like a million bucks and are ready to rock the world, everyone can expect a few tremors.

FIND YOUR AUTHENTIC STYLE

As you go through this chapter, you will find we are opinionated in our fashion do's and don'ts. Take this with a grain of salt as you work toward discovering what your authentic self likes or doesn't like, fashionwise. We have some particulars we are very adamant about, like avoiding bright blue seventies eye shadow and long acrylic nails, but we want you to put effort into developing your own style. Use this week to do just that: Develop an outward look that supports your inner Gal. As you go through this chapter, note which colors, styles, and fashion statements you are drawn to. Ask yourself questions to uncover your authentic style.

- Do you have certain clothing, jewelry, or accessories you've always admired and wanted to wear, but never had the gumption to put on? Why not make yourself up in an outfit from head to toe that would really define your persona rather than simply serve a practical purpose?

- Have you always wanted to wear sandals with rhinestones or cowboy boots or Birkenstocks, but never had the fire in your belly to just do it?

- Have you always wanted to dye your hair a particular color but been afraid to?

- Have you gotten haircuts based on what everyone else has rather than on what suits your own preferences?

- Have you tried not to stray from the SAHM uniform (same ol' T-shirt and sweatpants) that so many of the neighborhood moms wear?

- What clothes, accessories, hairstyles, and makeup do you wear simply to fit in?

Keep your answers to many of these questions away from the issue of money or expensive purchases. Whether you shop at Target, TJ Maxx, or Saks Fifth Avenue, these are questions to be directed not to your pocketbook, but to your inner, authentic style. You can be you without a huge bank account. Don't allow money to interfere with your image and inner self. This week work on bringing your inner character into your outer world by indulging those impulses and preferences that make you you.

One of our MomsTown ladies, Kellie, found that these questions helped her examine some patterns she had fallen into that did not speak to her authentic style. She addressed the question of jewelry, for example. "When I was young, and even in high school, I loved to wear several rings and bracelets at a time. I loved the sparkle and fun of all of the jewelry at once. One time, a really popular girl in seventh grade made a crack about how I looked like a gypsy and that all of the jewelry I had so lovingly collected at yard sales and consignment stores was tacky. Junior high was definitely one of the most formative periods of my life, and I reacted like I think most teen girls would. I quickly put most of the jewelry back in my jewelry box and began wearing only one or two pieces at a time, tastefully purchased and worn so as not to attract attention. As I was evaluating my personal style, I discovered that even though that happened in junior high, I still to this day remember that and hide my own sense of style. I am not being true to my authentic style on a daily basis because I don't want to stand out. I have made a habit, like so many people, of altering my style to fit in. Well, once I realized this, I began to collect jewelry, just like I had when I was a little girl. Right this moment I am wearing four bracelets and four rings, and I get compliments on them all of the time!"

Stay at Homework: Think back for a moment. Do you remember a time when you were criticized for not fitting in when you were being true to your authentic style? We at MomsTown encourage you to trust your authentic style and follow your fashion preferences when you dress, fix your hair, wear accessories. You will find that being true to yourself will set you free.

Stay at Homework: This week, choose an accessory, outfit, piece of clothing, or type of makeup you've always wanted to try but haven't. It doesn't have to be expensive. You'd be surprised what you can find at thrift stores, Target, or yard sales. As you shop, don't allow yourself to worry about what people will think.

The Assessment

Answer the following questions to see where you need to concentrate your efforts as you glam up your Gal.

Stay at Homework: Grab your diary and write answers to the following questions.

- What is your favorite color? Do you have a particular color that makes your eyes stand out? What colors make you glow and look vivacious when you wear them? These are your "key colors." Remember them when you are out shopping.

- What cuts in shirts, skirts, and pants flatter you?

- What body part have you always felt proud of? Do you have great arms, tummy, boobs, or a waist? Do you have gorgeous hair? Wonderful legs? A great butt? What clothes would accentuate this feature?

- What is your best facial feature? Your piercing blue eyes? Your pouty lips? Your button nose? What can you do to flatter it?

- What do you wear on a daily basis that brings out your best features?

- What compliments have you received that you always remember?

 • Do you like wearing dangly jewelry, or do you enjoy a simple, understated style?

Read back over your answers. This week try to begin making decisions on what you wear and what you think of yourself based on the strengths and features you feel good about. If you've always looked spectacular in green, wear green more often. Be aware of your beauty and do things to help it shine.

MomsTown Shower Power

We know this sounds obvious, but we must emphasize that something so simple as taking a shower can change your outlook on your day. Unless you are going to the gym first thing in the morning, we think you should be in the shower as soon as you're done making the bed. The fresh, new feeling you get when you step out of the shower is all the reason in the world. Make your bed, shower, and go through your Hot Iron prioritizing each morning.

Think of your shower as your own personal spa time each morning. Here are our secrets to a great shower. We want to give you things you can do to help you enjoy every minute of your shower. It is important that you take this time for yourself.

 • Make sure a cozy towel is waiting for you when you are finished.

 • Put some attention into your bathroom by making sure you have a plush bath mat to step onto after you finish showering.

 • The shower has to be warm but not too hot. Water that is too hot can dry out your skin and hair and break capillaries in your skin.

- You must have a fresh, invigorating shower gel. We recommend an orange, grapefruit, or mango fragrance, since these scents are terrific for waking you up in the morning. Lavender should be used during the evening bath or rinse. Try to stick to shower gel and avoid using soap. Most soaps dry out skin.

- Once you are in the shower, allow the water to heat your muscles and relax them. Position yourself so that the water is hitting your back and shoulders and slowly stretch your neck and shoulders as the water gently massages and relaxes you.

- Take a deep breath and clear your mind. Allow your body and mind to relax and fully feel the nurturing qualities a good shower can have.

- Notice how your senses are being awakened through smell, sound, and touch. Remember, this is your time this morning, before the kids and the schedule become your focus.

After you get out of the shower, you should get ready as if you are going to the office, even if you're just going in the kitchen to make the kids some breakfast. It's important to give attention to your appearance, as it assists in your mental preparedness and confidence—a perfect way to start the day. We don't want to hear excuses like "I always get dirty when I do dishes, make breakfast, lunch, dinner, or clean, so why take a shower and put on clean clothes?" That's what an apron is for! You have no excuse not to look your best. This means taking a shower or even a wonderful, indulgent bath depending on the amount of time you have.

Your routine after getting out of the shower should include the following:

- Putting on lotion, sunscreen, and body powder if you like
- Putting on makeup
- Combing your hair and getting ready to fuss a little (more on that in a minute)

These necessary steps after the shower provide a valuable structure and ritual each morning that bring attention to your image. Just as we asked you to do the first week of the program with making the bed, we also ask that you treat yourself well and pamper your body in the mornings. After you're finished, you'll feel ready for anything—except throwing on sweats and staying at home! You'll be a Gal who can go anywhere and is ready for anything, including tackling your new goals and showing off your new attitude and self-confidence. Getting rid of that grimy, unshowered feeling will set you up for your day in countless basic ways.

Remember, no matter how busy you are, you *can* do it. One of our moms, Becky, says of her routine, "I was told when I was pregnant that I would never have time to shower once the baby was born. Being a competitive person, I am proud to say that I have had a good shower and shaved my legs ninety percent of the time since my baby was born. Now, I may let other kinds of important things slide, but just because of the taunting phrase of 'you'll never shower again once your baby is born' ringing in my head, I make darn sure I get that shower and that I at least look pulled together each day."

Fuss a Little

We believe in fixing your hair in the mornings. At MomsTown, we encourage women to fuss a little. For some this may mean a period of time using a blow dryer, and for others it may mean a little product tossed in and you're good to go. Whatever your hair requires, the point is to give your hair its due. In paying attention to your hair, you give your appearance respect. Everyone who sees you will be inclined to do the same.

- Avoid simply pulling your hair into a ponytail each morning.

- Use product, even if it is just a bit of mousse or conditioner.

- Even if you like the "natural" look, treat your hair like you care about it.

If your kids are up, have them fix their hair while you fix yours—it's a great way to get them in the habit of taking pride in their appearance.

Make a point to fuss a little each morning. You will find yourself more prepared to meet the world, and the world will be more in awe of you.

Stay at Homework: Make a hair appointment once a month. As we said at the beginning of the chapter, it doesn't have to be at an expensive salon, it can be Supercuts. The point is to do this for yourself. It feels good to get your hair done, so make it a priority. Try a style you've never tried. Get highlights if you've never done it before. Take a risk (an educated one!) and see how it feels.

Sunscreen

No matter where you live and no matter what the season, it is imperative to protect your skin. Daily moisturizers often have an SPF built in, so it's very easy to get the protection you need. Make sure you apply sunscreen in the morning when you get ready. Blending this into your routine can take years off your face as you age.

Stay at Homework: If your moisturizer doesn't contain sunscreen, go out and get a new one this week and begin using it regularly.

> ♦ Hip Tip: Read the label on your moisturizer. Beware of products containing mineral oil. Mineral oil should not be put on your face. It doesn't let your skin breathe and it clogs your pores. There are many great botanically based skin care products on the market to choose from. ♦

Fingernails, Not Claws

We think women should avoid the time-consuming, money-eating habit of obsessive acrylic nail applications. The saying "less is more" definitely applies to fingernails.

A poll conducted by MomsTown among men shows they are not impressed with long acrylic nails.

After one of our MomsTown clients, Donna, heard our views on fingernails, she confessed, "I got attached to doing my nails each week and I quickly got bored with the basic manicure. I started getting acrylic nails and buying elaborate paintings for them in crazy colors. It was fun but expensive. I rationalized it as a gift I was giving myself. That was all well and good, but gradually this 'gift' nudged my gym membership money out of the picture until my workout became getting my nails done. I told myself that getting my nails done each week was 'taking care of myself.' This is true to an extent, but I began feeling that it made up for not going to the gym. I have now bought my own home manicure set and do my nails each week inexpensively and use the money I save to go to a local gym . . . where I've already lost five pounds! Not only is it helping me fit into clothes I haven't worn in years, but also I don't get jokes from my friends about my nails anymore. And my husband is happy; he never liked my long nails."

Stay at Homework: Begin taking time to buff and paint your nails at home each week. Treat yourself once a month to a manicure or a pedicure. If you are someone who gets a manicure every week, try doing your nails at home and see how you like it. If you can afford it in your budget, you can get your nails done by a professional once a month. If you are someone who never takes time to do your nails, try putting aside some time to do them. It can be fun!

Brighten That Smile

Not everyone is blessed with perfect pearly whites. Most of us have to freshen up our smile to bring back the shine. Today there are many products on the market to whiten teeth, from whitening agents in toothpaste and at-home whitening strips to customized bleaching trays from the dentist or one-hour laser whitening treatments. There is no reason not to have a sparkling smile. Check out your drugstore tooth-care aisle next time you're there. You may find some affordable whitening products that will have you smiling even more!

The point is *not* to look like the superbright smiles in a magazine, but to give attention to your smile. The better you feel about your smile, the more you will use it. We are not recommending expensive dental cosmetics—just small steps to improve self-esteem.

Flossing: Yoga for Your Teeth

If you have never flossed, if you always forget, or even if you do it only once or twice a week, we ask you to start doing it every day. We know we may sound like your dentist, but we promise you will feel a million times better if you do it. This is one health tip that will keep your smile, gums, and teeth in good health. It also serves to keep the nerves in your mouth awake and responsive, and it improves blood circulation in your gums, just like yoga does for your muscles.

You will feel terrific after you finish, and if you get your kids in the habit of doing it, you might save on dental bills.

Stay at Homework: If you don't do it already, begin flossing every day this week. Floss when it is most convenient for your schedule, but ideally before bed. There are many types of floss and flossing sticks that are easy to carry in your purse, leave in your car, and have at your fingertips when you need them.

Shape Your Face

Give your eyebrows some attention every month. Eyebrows frame your face and are a great way to clean up your appearance and widen your eyes. Giving your eyebrows attention can be done in a number of ways.

One option is to have your eyebrows shaped by a professional trained to do so.

Another option is to pluck your eyebrows yourself. Just be careful not to pluck too much. It's better to pluck too little than too much. It takes approximately sixty days for an eyebrow follicle to generate a new hair after it is plucked. And an eyebrow hair lasts about three to five months before it is shed. Since eyebrow hair does not grow back as quickly or dependably as the hair on your legs, it is best not to experiment!

Stay at Homework: This week, go ahead and do one of the above if you don't already give your eyebrows attention.

Make Up Your Gal

Makeup can be fun. If it doesn't feel that way to you, reevaluate what you think its purpose is. The MomsTown rule with makeup is, Less is more. We vote for the natural look. No one wants to look as if they're trying to mask their skin as it ages, no matter how tempted we all might be to do it. People can tell when a woman who wears too much makeup is trying to cover her perceived flaws. If one eats healthily, gets exercise on a regular basis, drinks plenty of water, and rests, a natural glow will make the aging process much more graceful. The more makeup you apply, the older you will look. There should be a balance. Use makeup to subtly enhance, not blatantly disguise.

Stay at Homework: Next time you go through your makeup routine, observe any excessive aspects that can be cut out of it.

Let's assess where you are with your present makeup routine.

- Do you feel as if you have to wear it? Try to think of makeup as fun to wear. Anything that feels like a chore *is* a chore! Think back to how much fun makeup was when you were a little girl. Reawaken your experimental self and don't become a slave to your same old routine.

- Is there a particular part of your makeup you feel you are supposed to use, like foundation or blush, and don't like using? Don't use it anymore!

- Do you feel your present makeup routine is stale? Get a makeover. They're free at most department stores. Do it with your buddy or a daughter if you have one.

- Do you have old tubes of makeup that are cluttering your makeup bag? Toss them after six months. Bacteria grows in them after that period of time, and that can't be good for your complexion.

- Does your entire makeup collection weigh down your purse? Don't carry unnecessary makeup in your bag. The two most essential items are lipstick and powder. The rest can stay at home. Not only do eye shadow and blush compacts break easily in your purse, but you don't need to apply them constantly.

- Do you want a shortcut to getting ready that has a two-step makeup routine for when you're almost out of time? Moisturize and wear lipstick. It's that easy. Even Grandma does it, because it gives her face immediate color and it's an easy way to keep up your looks all day. Instead of dark lipstick, we recommend you use a light-colored lip liner to shade your lips and then apply lip gloss.

Stay at Homework: Remember the new lipstick or lip gloss you purchased the first week of the program? It's time to try another one. Get a new shade of lip gloss or lipstick this week. Make it one you've never tried before.

YOU ARE WHAT YOU WEAR

We have already said we aren't in favor of the daily sweatpants look. We think you should look as good as you can, even when you're just home with the kids. In the first week we told you to go through your closets and drawers and weed out those things that bring you down, make you look drab, baggy, and not your best.

Constantly evaluating your wardrobe and the state of your closet and clothes and how these items speak to your new identity is an issue of maintenance, not a one-time thing. Now we'd like you to go through your closets and drawers again, looking for any clothes that don't speak to your new persona. Here's a handy checklist to use as you go. Some of these points were in Week 2, and we'll repeat them now:

Throw away anything you haven't worn in the last two years.

Be critical of clothes that are merely functional and that you don't particularly like.

Be leery of clothes that are not in your key colors.

Throw away any clothes with holes or tears.

Throw away any clothes that were gifts you've kept to be polite.

Throw away any clothes that do not fit—even your skinny jeans. (You can buy another pair when you shrink two pant sizes. Having those pants in your closet does more to clutter than motivate.)

Throw away any clothes that do not flatter you.

Throw away any bras and panties you would be ashamed if others saw.

Give all of your throwaways (even those in good condition) to a charity.

When dressing your children, keep the same rules in mind. Help them feel as good as they can in their clothes, too.

Next time you shop for clothes, remember the colors and clothes that make you feel alive, sexy, and put together. There are plenty of ways that you can shop for less and still look fantastic. Having a nice wardrobe has less to do with money and more to do with a discerning eye.

Make your wardrobe a part of your life that enables you. Don't allow your wardrobe to be a collection of unflattering outfits that weigh you down and make you feel dowdy when you are in public.

Accessorize Your Gal

Sometimes when we don't have time or money to buy a new outfit or to spice up our appearance, all we need is an accessory to make it work and feel new. Accessories include a whole host of items. Do you have a particular accessory you wish you could wear more often but don't because you think you don't need it for "just around the house"? Grab those accessories and have some fun with them, whether you are in the house, going to the grocery store, going to the park, or just making dinner. Some accessories to keep in mind: scarves, bracelets, earrings, necklaces, bags and purses, and shoes.

The most important thing to do is to make accessorizing fun. One of our moms, Tracy, said of getting rid of her diaper bag, "Instead of carrying both a purse and a diaper bag, I splurged on a beautiful large bag that doubles as both."

A few of our moms agree on the diaper-bag point. One of our moms, Tina, says, "I don't ever carry a diaper bag. I get a cool bag that will hold everything but doesn't make me look like I'm carrying around a portable nursery. A grown woman with Pooh Bear all over her accessories is not a hip thing." Be creative in whatever way speaks to your authentic style.

Just because you're a mom, you don't have to have it written all over everything you own. This brings us back to a key point of the Moms-Town program: *Define yourself as you see fit. Don't let your identity as a SAHM be your only defining characteristic.*

Stay at Homework: Make cleaning out your wardrobe your project for this week, even if you've done it once in the past month. Doing it again is a great way to further reduce the amount of things you don't need, and to remember the things you do.

Effort, Not Age, Matters

No matter how old you are, how much time you spend in the house rather than in public, or what habits you have become accustomed to, we urge you to make an effort to take care of your appearance. People will notice, and so will you!

WEEK 9 SUMMARY

1. Shower after making your bed every morning.

2. Continue to work out at least three times a week. Make sure you're pushing yourself beyond where you were when you began your workouts. Make a challenge for yourself.

3. Add something to your wardrobe or jewelry box this week that speaks to your authentic style. It can be from a thrift store, yard sale, or boutique. It doesn't have to be expensive.

4. Clean out your closet and drawers and make sure your wardrobe accentuates your new self and doesn't cover it up!

5. Give your makeup a makeover. Make sure you like what you put on your face.

6. Buy a new shade of lipstick or lip gloss.

7. Floss every day.

8. Put some time and effort into your eyebrows.

WEEK 10: POWERFUL AND POCKETS FULL: THE MOMSTOWN WAY TO MAKE, SPEND, AND SAVE MORE MONEY

This chapter is dedicated to the almighty dollar. We are going to share with you the MomsTown money philosophy, which includes how you can make money from home, why budgets are a bad idea, and why SAHMs are an economic force to be reckoned with. You are going to learn what you can start doing this week to turn your passion into profits.

OUR MONEY PHILOSOPHY

Money is important because it buys freedom. The traditional stereotype of a SAHM is a person who doesn't make money. We at MomsTown are changing that. It is possible to stay at home, take care of the kids, and create income for your family.

You know money is important. Money is important because it affords you the luxury of taking a class when you want to learn a new skill, sending your kids to college, or taking the family on an adventure. It buys you the freedom to put your family's needs first and the choice to live where and how you want to live.

SAHMs don't get a paycheck, which can sometimes mean we feel invalidated. Societies place emphasis on money as a form of reward and acknowledgment for a job well done. Many women spend their adult lives earning a paycheck—until they became SAHMs. Ironically, as moms we are doing the most important work of our lives (raising our children), but we get no monetary acknowledgment. Getting the occasional pat on the back from your husband or a thank-you from your four-year-old is sometimes not enough to make you feel as though you are being acknowledged for your work.

And as SAHMs ourselves, we understand the guilt you may feel when you spend money on yourself.

MomsTown has seen with countless moms that it is possible for you to earn a paycheck while not sacrificing your most important job, being a mom. We know the satisfaction of a parenting job well done—hearing your children giggle in the backyard while they play, seeing the wonder on their faces when they learn something new. This is what's great about being a SAHM: You don't miss any of the mommy moments. But there's another kind of job well done that some of us miss—the kind that means money in the bank.

The possibilities for you to make money out of your home have increased with technology. Technology has opened an entire new dimension to being a SAHM and is one of the vehicles that will help deliver your paycheck. Technology is key in changing the definition of what it means to be a SAHM and is bringing corporate America to your kitchen counter. You can make a sandwich for your child, take a conference call, and check your e-mail, all from the comfort of your home.

Your Passion Can Fill Your Pockets

In our program, we talk a lot about figuring out what your passion and interests are and taking them to another level—both personally and financially. If you can do this, money problems will begin to resolve themselves. "Do what you love and everything will fall into place," as the saying goes. Sharing this philosophy with our MomsTown members has brought us some very rewarding stories.

Lana, a mom of two children, found that cooking was her passion. Some might classify cooking as mundane labor that many SAHMs do not enjoy, but Lana found it to be very rewarding and discovered she has a terrific talent for it. Lana was having trouble making ends meet financially and decided to begin cooking for others. She now has a successful catering business. She became so successful she had to build a larger kitchen area in her house. Lana found following her passion fixed her money problems. She is a successful entrepreneur and now has enough business to hire assistants. She is happily doing what she loves while being at home with the kids.

You, too, can do what you love and make money. We have talked a lot about finding your passion. Now let's take that a step further. How can your passion bring you profits? If you focus on your passion unrelentingly, the rest will be taken care of. Pursuit of your passion can even be seen as financially responsible. All it takes is faith, devotion, and confidence.

Stay at Homework: Grab your diary and begin to plan how you will eventually turn your passion into profits. How can you make money doing something you love from home? For example, one of our moms, Beverly, is a gifted seamstress and made a beautiful custom crib set for her new baby. How could she sew her talent into dollars? She figured out how by starting a Web site that advertised her talents, attending craft shows and fairs, and selling her wares. Before she knew it, word of mouth produced loyal clients and a paycheck.

Another mom of ours, Lacey, makes incredible beaded jewelry, earrings, necklaces, and bracelets. How did she twist her artistic flair into dough? She began having open houses to showcase her jewelry and her whole local MomsTown chapter began attending and purchasing pieces.

Melanie, a loyal MomsTown member, is an administrative whiz. She can transcribe dictation, develop a Web site, and keep receivables ahead of the payables. How did Melanie parlay her own skills into deposits? She became a virtual consultant for some local businesses that asked her to analyze their offices and lend her organizational wisdom.

Stay at Homework: What are you good at? What type of work or play do you enjoy? You probably have a multitude of talents and skills. In this exercise we want you to list them all. The longer the list, the better. Try to see options rather than limitations in your own abilities. This is your opportunity to boast and get it on record. When you see a list of your skills on paper, you will begin to see how they might connect. Themes will begin to emerge.

Some of you already have a home business. We suggest you take this opportunity to figure out how you can make it bigger and more successful. How can you reach more customers or clients? How does this business suit your end-all dream and passion?

For others, this is the beginning of your business. Don't allow yourself to be overwhelmed. Take this time to dream and strategize. Choose what you believe you are good at and you enjoy. Then begin to do a little research. Be practical.

- Who is your competition?

- What are they doing to market themselves?

- How much are they charging?

- What makes your product and/or service unique?

- What do you need to make this work for you? A babysitter a couple of hours a week to begin with?

Once you've decided what it is you'd like to try, it's time to develop a business plan. This may seem like a big step, but it's not. Have faith and courage.

Stay at Homework: Go to MomsTown.com for a sample business plan and take it from there. Don't let yourself be discouraged. If you don't figure something out right away, train yourself to see everyday opportunities in your hobbies and interests, and something will emerge. Seeing your capabilities and the endless array of possibilities is a whole new way to look at the world. If an answer doesn't come to you right away, stay alert and persistent as you examine your life.

When you decide what you are going to do and how you will do it, treat it as a professional would. This is the same advice we've given you when we ask you to be loyal to your schedule, your home office, and your appearance—do the same for your passion and business. That means giving yourself credit, serious time, and devotion to develop your idea.

Here are some quick tips as you begin approaching your very own business:

- Don't let someone tell you your dream is a bad idea.

- Stick to your business plan and adjust it as you go.

- Don't act like a mom in your business. You are a professional.

- Expect success.

- Persevere and be persistent.

- Everything good happens in due time.

When MomsTown was still just a business plan, we had someone tell us that an Internet site for moms could not prove profitable. They could not have been more wrong!

Paycheck Ownership

If you're a SAHM who does not work out of your home, or even if you're just beginning to work out of your home and haven't yet achieved financial success, you have the dilemma of being responsible for a heck of a lot of work with no paycheck to show for it. Women don't get paid an hourly rate or a fee for what they do in the home. Often, both the wife and the husband fall into the trap of feeling that the woman doesn't have the same ownership of the paycheck because it has the husband's name on it.

Phooey. We disagree. *You share the paycheck.* If there is resistance on the side of your husband, you can calmly explain the fabulous deal of the century he is getting! Because you are home with the kids, they are healthy, strong, and vibrant, and he is able to go to work with peace of mind. Having peace of mind is invaluable. No one cares for your children like you do; no one loves your children like you do. He is able to afford the absolute best for his children, wife, and himself because you stay home and are helping him earn that paycheck. This concept is recognized in courts of law (and expressed in divorce settlements); you can recognize it in your home.

A good exercise is to sit down with your husband and discuss money values and their place in your relationship. Often, just opening the forum for discussion can lead to some discoveries that will surprise you. Just be sure to plan the talk ahead of time instead of springing it on him right after work unexpectedly or at the dinner table with the kids.

Here are some questions to get you started.

- Do you feel that we share your paycheck?

- Do you feel you give me an allowance out of your paycheck, rather than sharing the full amount with me?

- Do you feel you deserve more from your paycheck than I might because it is in your name?

- Do you feel the amount of money I spend from the paycheck ought to be itemized (spent only on household items or previously approved purchases), or do you trust my discretion on when and what to purchase?

- Do you ever feel I project resentment onto you because I don't get a paycheck myself?

By asking these questions, you can air any unspoken grievances and clear up misunderstandings before they happen. Communication is the most important component to keeping your marriage, relationship, and financial understandings strong with your husband.

One of our MomsTown members, Wanda, tells a story about lack of communication. "I had been stressed out about where we were going to get money for the kids' tuition in the fall. We had to pay it by a date that was fast approaching. I started worrying all of the time about it and found myself obsessing in the middle of the night. I was afraid my kids were going to have to change schools and they had just made friends in their new school. I couldn't stand the thought of them not going because we didn't have enough money. One night I lay awake for a couple of hours and finally woke my husband and told him how worried I was. He sighed and told me in a calm tone that he had just gotten a bonus last week, and that would cover the tuition. I wish I had related how stressed I was earlier—I would have saved so much energy."

As we've said, keep the lines of communication open. You never know what is not being communicated. It's essential you find solutions with your husband, and talking it out is the only way. Not only does the MomsTown program encourage you to put your attention toward making money doing something you love, but this week we will also go over some tips you can use to keep track of your money and make sure you're using it wisely.

Each mom finds financial techniques that work for her in terms of dividing paychecks and paying bills. One of our moms, Teresa, says, "My husband compares his long hours at work to my long hours at home and likes to believe I have it easy—but he won't stay home alone with the girls for more than a few hours. My sales consultant business helps a little bit from time to time with bills, but we're usually strapped. I take care of finances and bill paying. We call my husband's paycheck 'our paycheck' because a lot of the allowances the military gives him have to do with the fact that he's married and has two children. A little trick I learned from a budget counselor is to 'pay' yourself first, meaning when 'our paycheck' comes in, we give ourselves a portion of it first. It's usually a small portion, a hundred dollars, but we each get fifty dollars to spend as we please. We used to argue over crazy spending before we started doing this."

Why Budgets and Diets Don't Work

MomsTown doesn't believe in the traditional budget. Budgets make us feel deprived. No one wants to feel deprived, no one wants to feel that they can't buy things they want to buy, and no one wants to feel like they are being restricted in their spending. Instead of a budget, we propose a spending plan. A spending plan is a proactive plan that you and your husband put together. You decide what is most important to spend money on, rather than telling yourself what you are *not* allowed to spend money on. Allow yourself to focus on what you can spend rather than on what you can't. This simple shift in attitude puts a positive spin on your finances and your confidence.

We've talked about diets in week four and can all agree that they don't work in the long run. Diets and budgets are short-term solutions. The simple difference between being a "defensive spender" on a budget and being an "offensive spender" with a spending plan can make a world of difference. Your spending plan should empower you rather than limit you. The very act of seeing spending in a positive light instead of a negative light is amazingly freeing. Begin to find ways to make your money go further instead of dwelling on the limits of it. Let's try it with a few examples:

Budget: I can't go out to eat at the new, pricey restaurant tonight because I need to save money.

Spending Plan: I can go to the grocery store and buy enough groceries for the next week to make some really good dinners with some new recipes I've collected.

Budget: I can't buy that new outfit for the wedding coming up.

Spending Plan: I can wear a dress I already have for the wedding coming up and afford a pair of fun new earrings to liven it up.

Budget: I can't afford to go to the spa and get a facial, manicure/pedicure, and massage.

Spending Plan: I can afford to get a haircut and buy a new color of nail polish for my nails to give myself a manicure/pedicure.

If you continually focus on what you *can't* do (budget outlook), you will always feel limited no matter how much money you have. If you constantly focus on what you *can* do (spending plan outlook), you will always lead a full happy life—and you'll be less likely to splurge, complain, feel deprived and unhappy, and will keep your savings where they should be: in the bank or investments.

Stay at Homework: Make a spending plan today. Have a file in your home office labeled "spending plan." Organize it by week and month, up to six months. On a paper divided into weeks, denote the sum of money from the paycheck for each week and list the bills you must pay for that week. Figure out how much you have left over and what will go to savings.

Fifteen Minutes for a Financial Check-In

The financial check-in is one of the most important parts of managing your money. To every one of our MomsTown members, we strongly suggest a daily check-in with your finances for fifteen minutes. This is as important as making your bed each morning and doing your workouts. It's important to your peace of mind and your financial security. We know you can easily avoid dealing with your checkbook using your busy schedule as an excuse, but we believe strongly that this is an appointment that will make you saner, richer, and happier in the long run. Not knowing how much you have in your checking account or what bills are unpaid is a form of denial. Some may call it ignorant bliss.

Impulse purchases are harder to dismiss when you know how much you have in your checking account. Knowing the exact numerical figure that resides in your checking can rain on your parade at the shoe sale, give you the ease to make a great purchase at a surprise sale, and help you say a resounding no when you need to.

We promise that you will be a happier, less stressed person if you follow this advice: *Make it a habit to always know how much money you have.* As nice as that pair of pink mules would make you feel, knowing that you are already a few hundred dollars short in your account will help you walk away.

You won't overspend or avoid thinking about a bad financial situation if you check in for fifteen minutes a day. You may also be able to prevent a disastrous buildup of bills or mysterious balances. You can avoid time-consuming retracing of transactions you made a week ago. Below are some ways to spend your fifteen minutes.

- Balance your checkbook.
- Check your balance online.
- Pay your bills.
- Research investment opportunities online.
- File your important bills and receipts.
- Revise or update your spending plan.
- Check how many minutes you've used on your cell phone.
- Schedule on your calendar a year in advance when your bills are due.
- Once a week, make your fifteen minutes your Hot Iron. Do it when you find yourself more financially stressed than usual.

Even if you have time to do only one of the above each day, if you are consistent, you will never be in the dark about where your finances are.

You will have more confidence, you will be able to develop a knowledgeable spending plan, and you will never feel that panic of not knowing how much you have in your checking account or whether or not you can afford that cute dress. With fifteen minutes a day, you can save yourself money, time, and agony. You can no longer spend in ignorant bliss—you know exactly where you stand.

The Savvy GAL Shopper

We like to shop. Most people do. If you do, you don't have to give it up for your spending plan. You just need to recognize why you shop. Do you shop for the thrill of the kill? By this we mean:

- Do you shop to have something new to wear?

- Do you shop to give yourself a sense of renewal?

- Do you shop because you love the rush you feel when you find something you want?

We promise that you can get that thrill without overspending. We will show you a few ways how.

In our program, we have met many women who have a style or habit of shopping that bases decisions to purchase on emotional impulses rather than on the practical reality of their checkbook, or even on what a product is worth. Impulse buys happen when we feel harried, stressed, and underappreciated. They happen when we are on our way to run an errand or to purchase something we need and we see something we want.

Impulse buys are dangerous because they are not premeditated.

Before you make an unplanned purchase, mentally go through the following Savvy GAL Shopper checklist:

Do I really need this item? Think hard about what you have at home. Do you have something like this that you might have forgotten about? For example, one of our clients, Mindy, always found herself buying pink shirts, skirts, and pants. She would gravitate toward these items in a store because she liked the color, and she began making repetitive purchases of the same color and styles of shirts and skirts. One day she looked in her closet and realized she had four pink shirts! Does anyone really need that many of the same color shirt? Know what you own before you buy.

Walk away for at least a half hour and evaluate if you really need or want the item. Sometimes if we give ourselves a break from the pressure of a decision we can make a more objective choice. If you're at the mall, walk away, run an errand, and then make your decision. That orange-and-purple feather boa might not seem as attractive as it did a half hour ago, once you get away from the ambiance of the shop. If you leave and don't get a chance to go back, you can go back later in the week. If it helps, you may remind yourself that if you're meant to buy it, it will still be there.

Don't get bullied into purchases by manipulative salespeople. Remember, the salesperson who is complimenting you wants a sale! Without the salesperson telling you how fabulous it looks on you, how would you feel about the item? She won't be there to reassure you that those cheetah-print pants look sexy when you walk out of the house.

Don't purchase anything without knowing your exact bank account balance. Have you done your fifteen-minute financial check-in today? If you haven't, you need to avoid your impulse purchases.

Despite all of our cautioning, you deserve a treat once in a while. If you know how much you have in your bank account and if you don't

have a few other items just like it at home and you *love* it—go for it!
Don't deprive yourself all of the time. Use moderation in everything.
Feeling that you deprive yourself too often can eventually lead to a
splurge that will throw off your entire spending plan. If you go to the
extremes of avoiding buying a few small impulse items and staying on a
budget instead of a spending plan, you will eventually splurge, feel un-
dernurtured, and do some serious damage. Use common sense and treat
yourself once in a while.

Haggle Away

We love to negotiate and haggle. At MomsTown, we encourage it.
You'd be surprised how much fun shopping can be when you are not
buying something you can't afford. Instead, you are looking at things
that fit into your spending plan—and depending on your haggling skills,
it can be interactive. Here are some options for this.

- Outdoor sales
- Flea markets
- Yard sales
- Stores and boutiques that are personally owned
- Clearance sales
- Closing sales

Don't be shy! Offering fifteen dollars for a twenty-dollar item is
okay at yard sales or closing sales; in fact, it's empowering once you get
into the groove of haggling. And it's fun. It's a lot easier to get what you
want if you have a great attitude about it. Carrying cash for bartering at
craft fairs or yard sales is an easy way to persuade a vendor.

At privately owned stores or boutiques, if you are buying more than
one thing and are a frequent customer, sometimes you can say you'll

offer a lesser amount for a collection of things. If you find buttons missing or a snag that is barely visible on a blouse, ask for a discount and sew the button on yourself. The pride you will feel in your purchase will outweigh whatever imperfection it might have had initially. You're not being cheap—you're being smart. As you leave the store with a purchase that was 50 percent off, we can already hear you saying to your friend, "I got the best deal on this skirt!"

Shop Around

Sometimes moms don't feel they have the time to go around to all of the competitors and check competing prices simply to save a few pennies. The MomsTown program encourages its members to be savvy, calm, cool, and collected when shopping for that big purchase. You can save a good deal of money if you take the time to shop around. Do some research before you make a large purchase. By *large purchase* we mean:

major appliances (refrigerator, stove, washer/dryer)
cars
furniture and cabinets
bathroom fixtures (sink, tub, etc.)
ceramic tiles for floors and walls
computers
lawn mowers

Make time to do research. Taking time to do some investigating can save hundreds and even thousands of dollars. Here are some tips:

- Keep your excitement about making this purchase in check. Remember, this is a practical, analytical process—not an emotional one. Patience can save money.

- Visit competing stores.

- Surf the Internet. Depending on the item, you might even take time to look on eBay.

- Consult at least three vendors before deciding.

- Don't take anyone's word that "this is the best deal in town."

- Take the time to become an "expert" on the item you're purchasing.

- Check out our Web site. We have a few links that are perfect for the Savvy GAL Shopper in you.

Running through this checklist when you are about to make a large purchase is a good way to remind yourself not to be hasty. Nothing feels worse than buying a new computer and seeing it a week later for $500 less.

Pick Your Vanity Purchases

We all know there are things we would sell our minivans in order to have. Maybe it's a pair of heels that have been staring at you every time you walk by that storefront, a leather jacket that would transform your inner woman into a rock star, or a couch that you know would make everything painful in your life disappear every time you sat on it. These are what we call vanity items. They speak to your inner Gal, set off sirens in the spending plan, and make you incoherent and silly when you see them in a store. Beware of vanity items.

This is our advice: Acknowledge that these items exist and learn to discriminate. We are all (well, most of us at least) "material girls." Even if we are levelheaded about most things, we have weaknesses. Rather than banishing our material girl, let's train her!

Stay at Homework: Figure out what your vanity items are and make a list. We really recommend keeping yourself to one or two vanity items per every six months, depending on your financial situation and spending plan. The more carefully you pick, the more rewarding and less impulsive these purchases will be. Discriminate, plan, save, and buy quality over quantity.

Allow yourself to be proud of how you planned to buy these items rather than focusing on when you will get the next item. You will be much more grateful for a purchase made with planning and saving than an impulse buy that will leave your spending plan with a deficit.

Avoid allowing these items to carry emotional significance or have a role in remedying discontent. Know this: Buying these items will not improve your life. But if you buy with caution, while planning, saving, and discriminating, you set a great example for your kids and you will be empowered. The more you evaluate why and how you are buying these choice vanity items, the more satisfying they will be for you.

Save, Save, Save

The more you save, the more your children will understand how to save, and the more they will have for their future. As we always say, you are a role model for your children in everything you do.

Make a point to research financial strategies. If you haven't done it, meeting with a financial consultant is a good idea. Both you and your husband should go. The perspective an expert can lend on long-term investments, local real-estate trends, and customizing a plan for your family can be very helpful.

Stay at Homework: Make an appointment this week with a financial consultant, especially if you have never done it or it has been a while. Most of the appointments are free. You can only gain by doing it.

Do you have credit cards that reward you with frequent flyer miles or points? If not, do some research and make a plan to use the credit card for purchases and pay off the balance every month; that way your money is working for you twice! Eventually you and the whole family can fly on vacation somewhere for free. Be cautious, though—don't allow yourself to rationalize excessive spending through credit cards like these.

When you approach your finances in an empowered, confident lifestyle with short-term and long-term goals, you feel better about why you are using your money for one thing and not another.

Get excited about your financial options and opportunities and stop dreading them. Be creative, organized, and energized about becoming an empowered financial expert. Make your money work for you so your family can work less. Even if you have a dynamic spending plan now, there is always more you can know and do.

Stay at Homework: Make a list of your short-term and long-term financial goals. Be realistic. Make a category for each on paper and sit down with your husband this week to go over them.

For the short term, you can look at the plan in terms of weeks, months, and years. Short-term goals may include

- getting your hair done
- decorating a room

- buying some new pots and pans
- going on a vacation
- paying your children's tuition in preschool, a private school, or even college (if your kids are young, college can be a long-term goal)
- buying groceries
- paying doctor bills

For the long term, you can look at five to ten years, twenty years, and so on. These goals may include

- buying a home
- saving for retirement
- a large-scale renovation
- buying a new car

The very act of sitting down to lay out some of your short-term and long-term goals will help you figure out how much you need to save before you spend. Actively talking with your husband about these goals may reveal differences of opinion that are easier to sort out now than later. Planning can aid your bank account, your investments, and your relationship with your husband.

On our Web site we have some outstanding references for learning more about finances and how to handle your money. To do some in-depth research, take a look at our list of recommended books and Web sites.

Don't Knock the Piggy Bank

We think kids should have a piggy bank, and we think you should, too. It doesn't have to be a pig, of course; it can be a jar. Pocket change, change found on the floor or behind the couch, and tooth fairy gifts can help fill up the piggy bank for your kids. Nowadays, many supermarkets have machines that change coins into bills. Saving up for something you or your kids want in your respective piggy banks can be an adventure.

Stay at Homework: Make an event out of depositing money into the piggy bank if your children are young. Help them get excited about saving rather than spending. Even if you just give them small amounts of money in coins each week, make it a ritual. This week,

* allow them to choose their piggy bank (an actual bank or jar).

* make a project out of decorating it with them.

* emphasize that it is a special piggy bank that is for them and them alone.

* make an occasion out of their first penny in the bank.

* congratulate them on it.

By making a special effort to emphasize the responsibility of saving money, you can teach your children early on how important it is.

Take the Kids to the Bank

By making a point of giving your kids a piggy bank, taking them to the bank with you, and opening a savings account for them, you gently make finances something they learn to respect. Saving with a piggy bank should be an adventure, and so should going to the bank. We both take our kids to the bank with us and they each have a savings account. Many of our MomsTown members have begun doing the same. When Grandma or Grandpa gives them money for a holiday gift, we make depositing that money an adventure. By helping them immediately deposit the money, we are helping our kids feel empowered. As we teach them, we remind ourselves how important saving can be.

Stay at Homework: If your kids don't have a bank account, open one this week.

Other Ways to Save

There are other ways to save than a simple savings account. Savings accounts are the least aggressive, most passive ways to keep your money for the future. There are always new alternatives. This week, make a point to research some new options for your family and yourself. Continually educating yourself on financial options will keep you abreast of how your family can get ahead.

GAL-ercise: This week, spend at least a half hour online looking into all sorts of investments.

- Investing in a home (or second home)
- Adding on or remodeling your home to increase its worth
- Investing in mutual funds
- Creating your stock portfolio
- Subscribing to a financial e-newsletter

Think creatively about how to make your savings more significant as you research different ways to save and invest.

Financial Karma

Yes, we do believe in karma. We believe doing generous, selfless things will bring wealth to you. A wise woman said, if you hold water in your palm and tighten your fist, it leaks out. This is true for money. Being too frugal or too stingy will not bring you financial or spiritual wealth. If you are stingy in your wallet you are stingy in your heart.

We all know someone who disappears when the check comes or will gladly accept a round of drinks but never volunteers to pay for one. We also know that we are not usually inclined to invite this person out with us again! Giving to your friends, family, and others in acts of regular generosity will bring you wealth in the future. Wisely choosing a time to pick up the tab for lunch with a friend will pay off, and perhaps when you find yourself unable to pick up the tab, that karma will come back to you.

A great example of this happened one day when Heather was stopped in her car at an intersection and saw a man selling newspapers. Everyone at the traffic light was ignoring him and she decided to buy a newspaper. He thanked her and handed her the newspaper, mentioning that this was the only one he had sold all day. Heather happened to have a ten-dollar bill and decided spontaneously to give it to him. His smile was a reward unto itself. An hour later we got a call that Hyperion wanted to buy our book for publication. Believing this was merely a co-incidence would miss our point entirely. Good things come to those who are generous. It may not be as immediate as our story, but eventually it will happen. Just as we believe a positive outlook and proactive spending plan can lead to more financial security, we believe well-placed, balanced generosity and common sense can make you a rich person, both in life and in finance.

WEEK 10 SUMMARY

1. Make a spending plan this week.

2. Make a list of short- and long-term financial goals.

3. Do your fifteen-minute financial check-in every day.

4. Evaluate how you feel about paycheck ownership and discuss with your husband if necessary.

5. Be a Savvy GAL Shopper and ask yourself to evaluate your impulse purchases. Go through our checklist to avoid the pitfalls of impulse shopping.

6. Make a list of your vanity items and plan, discriminate, and pace yourself on buying them.

7. If they don't have one, get your kids a piggy bank and a savings account.

8. Make an appointment with a financial consultant to research new savings and investment plans.

9. Do one thing that will bring you financial karma this week.

CONCLUSION: THE MOMSTOWN WAY OF LIFE

Now that you've completed the program, you have earned some basic tools for making the MomsTown program part of your everyday lifestyle. If there is one wish we have for you, it is that you give your dreams the time and effort they deserve. Raising your family is a wonderful gift you have been given and so is the potential to achieve your dreams and live your life to the very fullest.

Make this book a part of your routine and use the discoveries you have made throughout the program to bring you closer to the Gal you want to become. You owe it to yourself to live up to your potential, treat your body respectfully, and be everything you can for your family. Remember, when you work toward getting it all, you work toward a better home and future for your family.

Just because this is the last chapter in this book doesn't mean Moms-Town won't be with you throughout the rest of your journey. We encourage you to reread this book, remind yourself of the principles you have chosen to live by, and participate actively in our online community. After all, MomsTown isn't just a program, it's a community and a way of life!

ACKNOWLEDGMENTS

From Mary:

To my husband, Bill, thanks for giving me room to be a dreamer and for believing in home runs. I love you big.

To Sterling and Portia, my darling daughters. My life truly began when you were born.

In memory of you, Dad, thank you for believing in everything about me. To Mom, for teaching me independence and that anything is possible. Thanks to the rest of my family, too, with a special thanks to Pam for keeping me hip and for styling the back of my hair, and to Peter for being MomsTown's techie-in-a-pinch.

Thank you, Margaret, for being a great mother-in-law, and to the rest of the Rendler family who welcomed me with tons of love.

To Allison for always pushing me to do more; to Chris and Jane for being true-blue friends; and to Stacie and Robert for always being ready to hit the road!

To Harry,

It was as if I was looking in the mirror the day we met. It was crazy to hear my dreams coming out of your mouth. We are opposites in many ways, yet the same. It's been a blast; brainstorming brilliant ideas, making scary calls, kids underfoot, popcorn, and Diet Cokes. You are the other half of my brain and a big part of my heart. Now, let's go make something happen!

Love, Meather

From Heather:

To my husband, Steve: Isn't it a relief to see this in print? Thank you for believing in me and my crazy dreams. You are the love of my life, to infinity and beyond! To my other three loves, Evan, Hayden, and Nolan, you make everything possible. To my mom, thank you for being a stay-at-home mom, and for teaching me compassion, independence, and how to laugh. To Dad, thank you for never missing a track meet or a softball game and for teaching me to always look for the pony. To my sister, Paige, you truly are my soul-sister.

I also would like to thank Grandma Askegreen for teaching me the value of family and friends, and my late Grandpa Askegreen for teaching me to live for today. To my Grandma Jennings, whose eyes reflect love, and to my late Grandpa Jennings, who always had a song in his heart.

It's a lucky woman who gets in-laws like mine. Ken and Judy, thanks for loving me like a daughter. To Catie, thanks for believing in Moms-Town when the foundation was being poured, and to Alison, thanks for being the first Big Breaker. To the rest of my family, a big group hug.

To my friends who are my family: Kim and Laura, I love you. To Julie, Grant, Cap, and Cecilia, you always have a seat at Thanksgiving. To Joe and Dana, you're in charge of bringing the risotto.

To Meather,

I couldn't have done it without you. Who would have thought my Internet twin lived only ten minutes away? It was meant to be. Here's to mochas and macchiatos, plain and peanut, and Jupiter. Thanks for staying on the line when the kids were screaming in the background. Thanks for being my Ethel and having the courage to throw your hands in the air when the ride got big and scary. I can't wait to see what other big thrills are around the corner.

Love, Harry

From both Mary and Heather:

A special thanks to the following people who have helped MomsTown become what it is and shape its future. Notably, we feel lucky to work with and thank our visionary editor, Kelly Notaras at Hyperion, for recognizing the revolution. Also, a special thanks to Zareen Jaffery and everyone at Hyperion for making this project a dream experience.

Thanks to Amy Hughes, our best gal and editor; our agent Joelle Delbourgo; Jana Collins; Mark LeBlanc; Joe Lesko; Cindi and Wendy at 2 Silent Partners for believing in the empire; and to Lee, Chris, Wade, John, and Marika at wsRadio.com for a microphone and radio home. Thanks to Lou Niles for strategic advice. Thanks to Melanie for everything. Plus, thanks to Erin for helping with the kids so we could write this book.

And a very special thanks to our listeners at MomsTown Reality Radio, our newsletter subscribers, and our online visitors. Thank you for believing in the inherent creative power of women. Thank you for knowing you *can* get it all and that you *deserve* to get it all. We wish you love, friendship, and success. You're always welcome in MomsTown.